Household Solutions 3

with

Green Alternatives

1500 Quick Fixes

Hundreds of Earth-Friendly Solutions for the Home and Garden

**Dedicated to Wade,
a person who makes this world a better place
just by being in it!**

Reena Nerbas

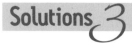

Household Solutions 3 with Green Alternatives
by Reena Nerbas

First Printing – April 2009

Published by Publishing Solutions, a division of PrintWest Communications Ltd.

Library and Archives Canada Cataloguing in Publication

Nerbas, Reena, 1967-

Household solutions 3 with green alternatives : 1500 quick fixes : hundreds of earth-friendly solutions for the home and garden / Reena Nerbas.

  Includes index.

  "Hundreds of green tips & earth friendly solutions".

  ISBN 978-1-897010-56-3

1. Home economics—Miscellanea. 2. House cleaning—Environmental aspects. I. Title. II. Title: Household solutions three with green alternatives.

TX158.N473 2009   640'.41   C2009-901761-X

Cover and page design by Brian Danchuk, Brian Danchuk Design, Regina
Cover photo by Inscho & Lindsey's Photography, Steinbach, MB
Editing by Kristen McLeod and Iona Glabus
Page formatting and Index by Iona Glabus

Designed, Printed and Produced in Canada by:
Centax Books, a Division of PrintWest Communications Ltd.
Publishing Co-ordinator: Iona Glabus
1150 Eighth Avenue, Regina, Saskatchewan, Canada S4R 1C9
(306) 525-2304   FAX: (306) 757-2439
centax@printwest.com   www.centaxbooks.com

Introduction

Though our grandparents kept clean and tidy homes without employing questionable products, that have nightmarish lists of health warnings; most of us are only now realizing that we can find much of what we need to maintain our homes within our very own cupboards.

While watching TV, have you ever stopped to count how many advertisements for cleaners and cosmetics there are? On average within a 1 hour period we are exposed to over 30 invitations to purchase toxic commercial solutions for our homes and bodies. We are a society obsessed with cleanliness. We want our teeth, towels, bathrooms and kitchens to be hospital white. Today's cleaning products promise faster, easier, better results and no scrubbing. Industry has answered, but at what cost?

More then ever before we understand that the chemicals we smear all over our children, our homes and our fabrics are simply not good for us. Is our obsession with cleanliness and increase of diseases such as asthma, respiratory problems, cancer, kidney and liver sickness just a coincidence? We sit on the couch and become convinced by advertisers that we need to kill every germ in our home and deodorize using fresheners that pollute the air we breathe. Companies are making billions of dollars each year but what is happening to our bodies?

Yes, changes are happening. Large corporations are beginning to realize that consumers want products that are healthier and more in-line with the expectations of the environmentally conscience consumer. With this in mind, some companies now label products "green," "natural" and "less toxic." Did you know that there are currently no legislations as to what is considered "green" or "natural"? If the bottle is green, the label can say "GREEN!" Consumers are duped by large companies into thinking that they are making healthier choices when in fact, sometimes the ingredients are less healthy.

The goal of this book is to encourage consumers to reduce, reuse and recycle. Be advised: Not every tip and solution in this book is "green." Some solutions are included just to make life easier. Other solutions tackle pests in ways that may not be in-line with "green" behavior, keeping in mind that creatures in our homes can pose a health risk to our family members and must be attended to.

Solutions 3

Following huge popularity from national best sellers, *Household Solutions 1 with Substitutions* and *Household Solutions 2 with Kitchen Secrets* it is with great pleasure that I present to you ***Household Solutions 3 with Green Alternatives!*** Hundreds of men and women from all over North America have contributed to this compilation of solutions. Included on the following pages are: all new recipes, hints, smart money saving tips and interesting trivia. Also included are gripping issues such as: Chemical Sensitivity, Greenwashing and cleaning product labeling from the CancerSmart Consumer Guide.

Toxic and non-toxic chemicals are everywhere. While we have come a long way since the Industrial Revolution, knowing when and how to properly use chemicals; we now recognize that they shouldn't be used for every household quandary we come across.

It's time for us all to wake-up and smell the chemicals!

Contact Information

Website: householdsolutions.org

Additional Quotes

"From the purchase of our first home, the birth of our three children, to our house in the country; Reena has had a solution for every spot, stain, and smell that has come our way. Her solutions are always simple, environmentally friendly, and consistently effective. I have come to trust her advice so much, that now whenever I am faced with a new 'stubborn something' my first thought is always 'What would Reena do?' This is a book, that everyone should have."
–Loraleigh Epp, Neepawa MB.

"When I was younger my mother used to slather vinegar on me whenever I'd had too much sun. I smelled like a pickle. I've always thought Mom's reasoning smelled a bit off, too. Oh me of little faith. After reading Reena's solutions, I now know that vinegar is an excellent remedy for soothing sunburns. You know how people 'Google' information? If you want inexpensive, environmentally-friendly answers to housekeeping problems, maybe you should 'Nerbas' them instead.
– Janet Stewart, *CBC News at 6* Anchor and fellow *Winnipeg Free Press* columnist

"At a time when we all want to be green, Reena knows how. I often wonder 'what is she thinking?' When I see some of her solutions, but they work. Buy two books, keep one handy and give the other one to your kids as a going away present."
– Gary Doyle, Talk Show Host, 570 News/Rogers Communications

Legend of Symbols:

 GREEN SYMBOL (the universal recycling symbol). When placed beside a solution in this book, the purpose is to bring attention to the reader that reducing, reusing or recycling practices are used.

 RECIPE SYMBOL: The solution incorporates a recipe, that you can make at home using household ingredients, thus keeping the use of chemicals to a minimum.

 GREEN RECIPE: The solution incorporates green practices as well as a recipe.

 TRIVIA: This is an extra-special bit of information that brings awareness to a particular topic.

Dish Soap and Detergents

Biodegradable dish soaps and detergents are recommended for all solutions in this book.

Acknowledgements

Special thanks to: Dan Marce, Iona Glabus, Kristen McLeod and staff at Centax; Wade Nerbas, Kyah Nerbas, Kristi Nerbas, Austin Nerbas, Jordan Nerbas, Margret Malaviya, Rekha Malaviya, Sharon Nerbas, Garry Nerbas, Esther Bast, Sheila Kolesar, Jan Cooper, Joel Gosselin, Cindy Penner, Trish Jackson, Sandra Madray and Sean Grffin of Terra Choice Environmental Marketing Inc.

Also, special thanks to Kelly Taylor and the *Winnipeg Free Press*, who first printed selected "Solutions" lists.

Solutions 3

Table of Contents

Solutions 3

Table of Contents

Solutions 3

Dirty Secrets about Germs and Bacteria!

Today more and more cleaning products are advertised as exceptionally effective while requiring very little elbow grease. Just aim, gently pull the trigger and that's it – the soap scum, mold and germs disappear. Many people do not realize that cleaners often contain toxic, dangerous man-made chemicals and pesticides. Whatever happened to the cleaners of the past – vinegar, baking soda and olive oil?

TAKE THIS TRUE/FALSE QUIZ!

True or False: **The number one way that germs get passed is through improper hygiene.**

Answer: Sick of hearing it but it's TRUE. Wash your hands thoroughly before cooking, after touching raw meat, fish or chicken and especially after visiting the bathroom. Most food borne illnesses are related to improper hand washing after going to the bathroom. If hand washing facilities are not available, wet napkins or sanitizers will reduce the germs on your hands but won't eliminate them.

True or False: **The best way to prevent food poisoning is to eat many, many unwashed apples?**

Answer: FALSE. Raw meat and poultry, eggs, fish and unwashed fruit and vegetables can all carry germs. Thoroughly cooking food and performing scrupulous kitchen clean-up are the primary ways to prevent food poisoning.

True or False: **People who use strong toxic chemical cleaners to sanitize their homes are preventing themselves from ever getting sick.**

Answer: FALSE. Remember the words germs fear most: **regular soap and water. I can't stress it enough**! Washing your hands well is the best way to beat these tiny warriors. Wash your hands every time you cough or sneeze, before you eat or prepare foods, after you use the bathroom, after you touch animals and pets, after you play outside and after you visit a sick relative or friend. Use tissues for your sneezes but don't just throw tissues on the floor to pick up later. Toss them in the trash and, again, wash your hands!

Note: Even if a person chooses to use strong toxic chemicals to clean their homes and hands, how long would it take before germs are again present? Seconds! We aren't meant to live in a completely sterilized environment; in most circumstances people need germs to fight germs.

True or False: **Germs are found mainly in the homes of people who rarely clean.**

Answer: FALSE. Germs are found ALL over the world, in all kinds of places. There are four major types of germs: bacteria, viruses, fungi and protozoa. They can invade plants, animals and people and sometimes they make us sick.

True or False: **Cutting boards need to be kept clean.**

Answer: Please tell me that you said TRUE. We may not need to go overboard on cleaning the entire house but cutting boards, if not sanitized properly, may pose a problem. Cutting boards can harbor harmful bacteria in cracks and knife grooves, particularly after cutting meat or poultry. A good procedure for disinfecting both wood and plastic cutting boards, as well as other surfaces and utensils, is to spray them first with a mist of vinegar, then with a mist of 3% hydrogen peroxide. This combo kills bacteria on meat without hurting the food. Vinegar still does a great job at cleaning without leaving harmful residues on toilet seats and countertops.

True or False: **It is always best to purchase antibacterial cutting boards.**

Answer: FALSE. Beware! Last year, the EPA ordered two companies to stop selling cutting boards that carried labels claiming they prevented the growth of food poisoning organisms, including salmonella and E.coli and reduced the danger of bacterial contamination. These cutting boards had been treated by a pesticide that protects products from odor-causing bacteria but this agent has not been shown to be effective against organisms that can cause disease.

True or False: **Toilet seats contain more germs than anywhere else in the home.**

Answer: FALSE. According to studies done by the University of Arizona, the following objects are the biggest collectors and spreaders of germs: telephones (especially cell phones), desktop surfaces, keyboards, computer mouse, fax machines, photocopiers and toilet seats in that order. Cell phones are worse than desk phones because they are often kept in nice, warm pockets, which is the perfect environment for germs to breed fast. Since germs are passed from our hands as we touch things and, since we continually touch the phone, cell phone, keyboard, mouse and tops of our desk, we continually move the germs from one place to another.

 According to recent studies, cellphones have 400 times more germs than toilets.

Dirty Secrets about Germs and Bacteria!

Solutions 3

True or False: **Combining chemicals can be dangerous.**

Answer: TRUE! Most household cleaners contain toxic chemicals. Ammonia is in many of them and is lethal if combined with bleach (forming chloramine).

True or False: **Life would be better without bacteria.**

Answer: FALSE. No, no, no! Many large companies would love for everyone to think this statement is true but ridding ourselves of bacteria is a hopeless endeavor. Bacteria outnumber human cells in your body 10 to 1 and this is a good thing.

True or False: **All bacteria are harmful.**

Answer: FALSE. Bacteria are single celled organisms visible only with a microscope. They are so small that if you lined up a thousand of them end to end, they could fit across the end of a pencil eraser. Not all bacteria are harmful. In fact, less than 1% cause disease and some bacteria that live in your body are actually good for you. For instance, Lactobacillus acidophilus – a harmless bacterium that resides in your intestines – helps you digest food, destroys some disease-causing organisms and provides nutrients to your body.

True or False: **Life would be better if everyone used antibacterial soap all of the time.**

Answer: FALSE. Numerous studies show that antibacterial soap is no more effective than ordinary soap in cleaning your hands. Either kind lifts off germ-laden dirt. But antibacterial soap kills helpful bacteria on the skin, freeing up valuable real estate so that harmful bacteria can move in later.

True or False: **Triclosan is the answer to a cleaner life.**

Answer: You be the judge. Over the last two decades, antibacterial products have swarmed the marketplace, showing up in hundreds of different products, in everything from soaps and toothpastes to clothes, kitchenware and toys. In fact, a study done in 2000 found that over 75% of liquid soaps and nearly 30% of bar soaps – 45% of all the soaps on the market – contain some type of antibacterial agent. The most common active ingredient was Triclosan. A study of over 200 healthy households found that households using antibacterial products did not have any reduced risk for runny noses, coughs and other symptoms of infectious diseases. According to the American Medical Association, "Despite their recent proliferation in consumer products, the use of antimicrobial agents such as Triclosan in consumer products has not been studied extensively. No data exists to support their efficacious when used in such products or any need for them."

True or False: **Every cleaner on the market is thoroughly tested and appropriately labelled for safety.**

Answer: FALSE. Companies are protected by an old law known as "Trade Secrets." The law does not require companies to list all the ingredients of a product on a Material Safety Data Sheets (MSDSs). MSDSs are only required to list ingredients with acute and chronic health hazards. Chemicals are tested for their individual health effects. Few chemicals have ever been tested for their combined health effects on women and children.

True or False: **Household cleaners are safe – it's not like they can penetrate through skin.**

Answer: FALSE. Human skin is remarkably porous and will absorb many substances it touches into the bloodstream. We also ingest cleaner chemicals when we use these products or touch residues left on surfaces and then eat or put our hands to our mouths. Food itself is easily contaminated by cleaners or air fresheners used in the kitchen and cleaner vapors and tiny droplets suspended by sprays are invariably inhaled.

True or False: **According to the EPA, indoor pollution is no more polluted than outdoor.**

Answer: FALSE. According to the EPA, indoor air is 2-5 times more contaminated than outdoor air. Not only do chemicals pollute the air that we breathe inside, they leach onto our counter tops, floors, carpets, bathtubs, sinks and walls.

Note: Like cleaners, air fresheners are not regulated by the federal government and once again, companies are not required to list ingredients on their labels. Consumers should be wary of all air fresheners, even those that claim to be "all-natural" or made with essential oils. NRDC and other groups are petitioning the EPA and the U.S. Consumer Product Safety Commission to do additional comprehensive testing and to take action to protect the public from dangerous chemicals in air fresheners.

Solutions 3

Cleaning Products – Taking a closer look at the Ingredients

By Sean Griffin

It seems contradictory: cleaning products are intended to make our indoor environment cleaner – how can any of them be toxic?

Many people wondered the same thing when the Labour Environmental Alliance Society (LEAS) first began researching cleaning products used in a number of workplaces in B.C. In a LEAS-initiated project called Cleaners, Toxins and the Ecosystem, researchers reviewed Material Safety Data Sheets for hundreds of cleaning products to identify those that contained toxic ingredients. Then they worked with workplace health and safety committees to replace toxic cleaners with safer, environmentally-preferable alternatives. LEAS was awarded a pollution prevention award from the Canadian Council of Ministers of the Environment for its work in eliminating cleaners containing carcinogens and endocrine disrupting chemicals from schools, industrial worksites and other facilities. The project work is continuing on additional sites in Canada.

But it's much more difficult for consumers to know what to use, especially when most of the cleaning products available on the retail market offer no information on the potential long term health effects that might be associated with those ingredients.

Some environmentally-friendly consumer products such as those manufactured by Seventh Generation, Nature Clean and Ecover, do make it a practice to disclose their ingredients, setting an example for what should properly be the industry standard.

Consumers should have the right to know what toxins they may be exposed to in the products they buy. We're not there yet, but informed consumers can make a big difference in bringing about that change.

The best place to start in learning about what you're using is product category. There certainly are expectations, but most hand soaps and liquid dish detergents are fairly safe, for example. So are fabric softeners, although some people do experience allergic reactions to them.

Other products can be quite variable. Laundry soaps, for example, may contain trisodium nitrilotriacetate, or NTA, which is a possible human carcinogen and an environmental hazard. Some specialty products may contain ethoxylated nonyl phenols, which are endocrine disruptors. A few powdered abrasive cleaners contain silica, a carcinogen.

The products to check particularly carefully for hazardous ingredients such as carcinogens and reproductive toxins include carpet stain removers, floor strippers, tile cleaners and graffiti removers.

HOW DO YOU CHECK INGREDIENTS?

First, check the product label. Although there's usually not much ingredient information there, ingredients such as the carcinogen perchloroethylene and the reproductive toxins xylene and toluene or 2-butoxyethanol may be listed as ingredients. Avoid using these products.

Many product labels have a 1-800 number that consumers can call with questions and comments. Call that number and ask for a Material Safety Data Sheet. The more that people phone up and ask for MSDS, the more quickly companies will get the message that consumers want that information on the label.

© CancerSmart 3.0 The Consumer Guide. Reprinted by permission. Copies available at **www.toxicfreecanada.ca**

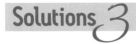
Solutions 3

DON'T BE FOOLED – BE INFORMED!

A Study of Environmental Claims in North American Consumer Markets. *A Greenwashing Report* by TerraChoice Environmental Marketing Inc. (November 2007) Printed with permission.

OVERVIEW

The recent surge of environmental awareness in North America is unmistakable. It has been documented by many researchers and widely reported in the popular press. The rise in "green" marketing claims has also been well documented. Less studied is the apparent increase in "greenwashing" – false or misleading green marketing claims.

In an effort to describe, understand and quantify the growth of greenwashing, TerraChoice Environmental Marketing Inc. conducted a survey of six category-leading big box stores. Through these surveys, we identified 1,018 consumer products bearing 1,753 environmental claims. Of the 1,018 products examined, all but one made claims that are demonstrably false or that risk misleading intended audiences.

Based on the survey results, we identified six patterns in the greenwashing, which we now recognize as the "Six Sins of Greenwashing™".

These findings suggest that greenwashing is pervasive, the consequences of which are significant:

- Well-intentioned consumers may be misled into purchases that do not deliver on their environmental promise. This means both that the individual consumer has been misled and that the potential environmental benefit of his or her purchase has been squandered.

- Competitive pressure from illegitimate environmental claims takes market share away from products that offer more legitimate benefits, thus slowing the penetration of real environmental innovation in the marketplace.

- Greenwashing may create cynicism and doubt about all environmental claims. Consumers – particularly those who care most about real environmental progress – may give up on marketers and manufacturers and give up on the hope that their spending might be put to good use. This would eliminate a significant market-based, financial incentive for green product innovation and leave committed environmental advocates with government regulations as the most likely alternative.

Of the 1,018 products reviewed, ALL BUT ONE committed at least ONE of the Six Sins of Greenwashing.

The "Six Sins of Greenwashing™"

1. Sin of the Hidden Trade-off: Was the most frequently committed sin in the study. A product such as this will cite a single attribute or narrow set of attributes as proof of greenness while ignoring other important environmental impacts. Examples are bathroom cleaners that claim to be chlorine free but may contain other toxic ingredients.

2. Sin of No Proof: Any environmental claim that cannot be substantiated by easily accessible supporting information, or by a reliable third-party certification, commits the Sin of No Proof. Household lamps and lights that promote their energy efficiency without any supporting evidence or certification. Personal care products (such as shampoos and conditioners) that claim not to have been tested on animals, but offer no evidence or certification of this claim. Facial tissues and paper towels that claim post-consumer recycled content without providing evidence.

3. Sin of Vagueness: Claim that are so poorly defined or broad that its real meaning is likely to be misunderstood by the intended consumer. There are some recurring themes within these vague claims. For example: "Chemical-free". In fact, nothing is free of chemicals. Water is a chemical. All plants, animals and humans are made of chemicals as are all of our products. "Non-toxic." Everything is toxic in sufficient dosage. Water, oxygen and salt are all potentially hazardous. "All Natural." Arsenic is natural. So are uranium, mercury and formaldehyde. All are poisonous. "Green," "Environmentally friendly," and "Eco-conscious" (to name just a few) which are utterly meaningless without elaboration. Some product examples from the research: Garden insecticides promoted as "chemical-free". "Natural" hair mousse. Kitchen (wax) paper that claims "recycled content" but does not quantify it (Would 0.1% qualify?). General purpose household cleaners that claim to be "non-toxic" without explanation or third-party substantiation. "100% natural" bathroom cleaners.

4. Sin of Irrelevance: Committed by making an environmental claim that may be truthful but is unimportant and unhelpful for consumers seeking environmentally preferable products. It is irrelevant and therefore distracts the consumer from finding a truly greener option. The most frequent example of an irrelevant claim relates to chlorofluorocarbons (CFCs) – a principal contributor to ozone depletion. Since CFCs have been legally banned for almost 30 years, there are no products that are manufactured with it.

Nevertheless, we found many individual products that presented CFC-free claims as an apparently unique environmental advantage. They included: CFC-free insecticides, CFC-free lubricants, CFC-free oven cleaners, CFC-free shaving gels, CFC-free window cleaners, CFC-free disinfectants.

5. Sin of Lesser of Two Evils: These are "green" claims that may be true within the product category, but that risk distracting the consumer from the greater environmental impacts of the category as a whole. Examples include: Organic cigarettes. "Green" insecticides and herbicides. Obviously, there are some circumstances and consumers that demand these products. Commercial insecticides and herbicides are essential to some agricultural applications. In those circumstances, choosing the greenest option is essential. However, insecticides and pesticides may be unnecessary for many cosmetic applications (such as lawns). Organic tobacco may be a more responsible choice for smokers, but shouldn't most consumers be discouraged from smoking in the first place? We consider a claim to commit the Sin of Lesser of Two Evils when environmental qualifiers such as "organic" or "green" are placed on products in which the entire product category is of questionable environmental value.

6. Sin of Fibbing: Committed by making environmental claims that are simply false. In our findings, only a few products were found to commit the Sin of Fibbing. Most of these were misuse or misrepresentation of certification by an independent authority. These cases included, for example: Several shampoos that claimed to be "certified organic", but for which our research could find no such certification. A caulking product that claims to be "Energy Star" registered, but the official Energy Star website suggests this is false. A dishwasher detergent that purports to be packaged in "100% recycled paper," and yet the container is plastic. CFCs have been legally banned for almost 30 years, yet many products still claim CFC-free as if it is a unique competitive advantage.

Governments and standard-setting bodies have attempted to discourage green-washing. In North America, both the US Federal Trade Commission and the Canadian Consumer Affairs office have issued guidelines for proper use of environmental claims. Under ISO 14024, the International Organization for Standardization establishes guidelines for proper use of environmental infor-mation. But it is our observation that when environmental interest is high, as it is today, greenwashing is nevertheless prolific.

If the good intentions of consumers and the environmental benefits of their choices are not to be squandered, consumers themselves will have to play a role. Here are some suggestions that arise from this study.

LOOK FOR ECO-LABELS.

Eco-labelling – standardized by ISO 14024 and recognized around the world – arose as an answer to earlier efforts of greenwashing. They remain one of the most useful tools to avoid greenwashing. Look for products that have been cer-tified by a qualified and independent third-party such as EcoLogoCM or Green Seal. Both EcoLogoCM and Green Seal develop standards for environmental leadership in an open, transparent consensus-based process that considers multiple environmental issues throughout a product's lifecycle (from resource extraction to end-of-life).

The Six Sins of Greenwashing does NOT suggest that only perfectly "green" products should be marketed as environmentally preferable. First of all, there is no such thing as a perfectly "green" product. Environmentally preferable prod-ucts are "greener" not "green" and marketing them as such is entirely fair. Second, environmental progress is necessarily stepwise. Not only should incre-mentally "greener" innovations and products be encouraged, consumers should and will reward stepwise progress.

Avoiding greenwashing does not require waiting for a perfect product. It does mean that sound science, honesty and transparency are paramount.

This excerpt was taken from TerraChoice Environmental Marketing's "Six Sins of Greenwashing" report.

Are you curious about the results? Interested in learning more? Would you like to speak to anyone at TerraChoice?

Please visit **www.terrachoice.com/sixsinsofgreenwashing** for more information.

Chemical Sensitivity

Multiple Chemical Sensitivities (MCS) is a medical condition characterized by debilitating chemical sensitivities. People who are chemically sensitive are made sick by exposures to chemicals found in many common products such as pesticides, perfumes, tobacco smoke, new carpets, air "fresheners," new paint and building materials and many cleaning and laundry products. Most of these chemicals will make everyone sick at high levels, but for chemically sensitive people exposures to even small amounts of these substances can cause symptoms. Some chemically sensitive people are only mildly affected while others have the more severe form of the illness called MCS.

Reducing exposures to chemicals improves the health of those with MCS. Better air quality also helps promote the health of everyone. The following are ways to create a healthier environment:

- Avoid pesticides, use the least toxic integrated pest management (IPM).
- Avoid newly built or remodeled buildings, or build with less toxic materials.
- Avoid new paint and solvent-based stains and transparent finishes.
- Avoid new carpets.
- Avoid gasoline, solvents, dry-cleaning and tar fumes.
- Avoid tobacco smoke and vehicle exhaust.
- Use the least toxic, natural and unscented cleaning, laundry and sanitizing products.
- Avoid perfume, cologne and scented personal care products.
- Avoid air "freshener" sprays, incense and fragrance-emitting devices.
- Use electric utilities or radiant heat.
- Open windows, ventilate buildings with clean fresh air and/or use portable room air filters.

Information taken with permission from the New Mexico MCS brochure which appears on the CSF website. For more information contact: Multiple Chemical Sensitivities-Task Force of New Mexico P.O. Box 23079, Santa Fe, NM 87502

AUTHOR'S NOTE: Multiple Chemical Sensitivities is not a cut and dry sickness; it is very controversial. Although chemical sensitivity is generally accepted as a reaction to chemicals the debate is whether or not MCS should be classified as an illness. The following is a list of some of the symptoms related to MCS: difficulty breathing, skin irritations, hives, headaches, nausea, seizures and anaphylactic shock. Contact your physician for a complete description of symptoms.

Thank-you to Trish Jackson for contacting me about the importance of addressing MCS and to Sandra Madray for her extensive information on the subject.

THE THREE R's – Reduce, Reuse and Recycle

Let's face it – we all produce garbage, and we are all part of the problem. The good news is that we can also be part of the solution. Studies show that 65% of "garbage" can be recycled or composted instead of tossed. Instead of throwing away items we no longer need, why not make sure they find their way to the next stage in their life cycle?

 Did you know? 17 million Canadians (nearly one third) have access to recycling.

Reduce: Every person creates an average of 4.6 lbs. (2.08 kg.) of waste per day, almost double the amount created 35 years ago. Reducing the amount and the toxicity of the waste discarded is the preferable method of waste management. Reducing is easy! Buying bulk, purchasing longer lasting products and demanding that manufacturers use less packaging for non bulk items are simple ways of reducing waste.

Reuse: Before throwing household items away consider another use for them. For example, a scratched CD makes a great reflector. Get creative or donate items you no longer want to charity and community organizations. Reusing is a step above recycling because less waste all together is produced.

Recycle: According to the Environmental Protection Agency (EPA) in 1999, recycling, including composting, diverted 64 million tons of material from landfills and incinerators. The benefits of recycling include conservation of resources, prevention of greenhouse emissions and other pollutants, saving energy, creating jobs, stimulating development of greener technologies and reducing need for landfills.
Tip: Buy products that contain recycled materials.

 Did you know? Since 1986, the average weight of soft drink cans has been reduced by 33% and 2 L plastic soft drink bottles went from 2.4 oz. (68 grams) of plastic per bottle to 1.8 oz. (51 grams), saving 250 million lbs. (113 kg) of plastic per year!

A terrific website to check out is **Environment Canada's** – Take Action site at **www.ec.gc.ca** – go to the **What You Can Do** link to the right.

To save water: Install low-flow toilets and shower heads; fix dripping faucets or update plumbing; collect rainwater in a rain barrel to use on all plants; install solar collectors which use the sun's energy to heat water used in your home; add a tankless water heater, which heats water only when you need it.

To save power; use a clothesline to dry clothing; install solar panels which collect energy from the sun and convert it to electricity; switch incandescent bulbs to CFLs; install a programmable thermostat; choose Energy Star® qualified major appliances; properly insulate your home with a higher R value can reduce energy use; unplug electrons that continually drain electricity when not in use; install ceiling fans to limit air conditioner and heater usage.

To save our earth; choose organic foods to reduce carbon dioxide emissions by up to 68%. See **coolfoodscampaign.org**; plant a native garden; reuse and recycle all containers; compost to create fertilizer for the garden; consider packaging – carry tote bags to avoid the need of plastic bags and use biodegradable bags for garden and household waste.

Be sure that your area has a recycling program and that you know which materials are accepted locally; then get the appropriate recycling containers. In some areas, plastics, paper, and glass go into separate containers. All three containers, along with garbage that cannot be recycled, is picked up by the local sanitation or recycling program. As well, recycle your food waste products by starting a compost heap.

One big change you could make is to take a look at the things you throw out. Thrift stores will take old furniture, clothing, household items, toys and accessories. Your community also may have a center for collecting salvaged building materials such as old sinks, carpet, carpet pads, lumber, screen doors, cabinets, plumbing fixtures, paint and more. Certain charities will even take old cars, eye glasses, computers and cell phones. Newspapers can be donated to the Humane Society.

DID YOU KNOW? Five recycled 2 L plastic bottles make enough fiberfill for a ski jacket.

DID YOU KNOW? Each recycled aluminum can saves enough electricity to run a television set for 3 hours.

Household Superstars

To be considered a Household Superstar in the *Household Solutions* series, a product must have effective uses beyond its original intention. Open up your cupboard doors and meet some of the best!

* **Cornstarch**
* **Mayonnaise**
* **Tea Tree Oil**
* **Toothpaste**
* **Vodka**

* Featured in *Household Solutions 3 with Green Alternatives*

* **Aspirin**
* **Baking Soda**
* **Borax**
* **Bread**
* **Cabbage**
* **Cinnamon**
* **Citric Acid**
* **Coffee**
* **Cola**
* **Glycerine**
* **Honey**
* **Hydrogen Peroxide**
* **Ketchup**
* **Kool-Aid**
* **Lemon Juice**

* **Mayonnaise**
* **Mustard**
* **Olive Oil**
* **Onions**
* **Peanut Butter**
* **Peppermint Oil**
* **Rhubarb**
* **Salt**
* **Shaving Cream**
* **Tea**
* **Vanilla**
* **Vinegar**
* **Washing Soda**
* **WD-40**

* Featured throughout *Household Solutions 1 with Substitutions* and *Household Solutions 2 with Kitchen Secrets*

Solutions 3

Household Superstar ... Cornstarch

What is cornstarch? Sometimes called corn flour, cornstarch is the starch of corn. It is ground from the endosperm, or white heart, of the corn kernel. Cornstarch is great for thickening gravy but that isn't all it's good for!

 Carpet Freshener Recipe: Combine ¾ cups (175 mL) baking soda, 2 tbsp. (30 mL) cornstarch and ¼ cup (60 mL) perfumed talcum powder. Sprinkle on dry carpet, let stand 5-15 minutes; vacuum.

 Extra-Shiny Windows: Clean windows as normal, then put cornstarch in a pail with water (enough to soak a cloth). Wipe the windows and dry with a clean cloth. *Submitted by Tina from Corner Brook, Newfoundland*

Shine Your Car: For extra shine, when buffing your car, sprinkle 1 tbsp. (15 mL) cornstarch onto a damp rag and buff.

• **Cockroach Poison**: Mix equal parts cornstarch and plaster of Paris. Sprinkle the mixture into cracks and crevices. Cockroaches will eat the mixture and won't survive.

 Prevent or Kill Mildew in Damp Books: Sprinkle cornstarch throughout books to absorb the moisture from damp pages, wait several hours and brush clean. If pages have mildew, brush the cornstarch off outdoors to keep the mildew spores out of the house.

 Cure Athlete's Foot: Sprinkle cornstarch on feet and in your shoes to absorb moisture, deodorize and reduce friction.

 Water-Free Dog Bath: Sprinkle cornstarch onto dog's fur and rub vigorously; then brush. The cornstarch will absorb dirt and oils from your dog's fur. This works on human hair as well but hopefully no one in your family refuses to get into the tub.

 Fresh Grease Spot on Fabric: Sprinkle cornstarch onto fabric and leave for a few hours. Brush off and wash with detergent and water. Make sure grease spot is gone before transferring fabric to the dryer.

 Make Your Own Glue: Mix 3 tsp. (15 mL) cornstarch for every 4 tsp. (20 mL) cold water. Stir until a paste consistency is reached. Apply with fingers, a wooden tongue depressor or a Popsicle stick.

 Fantastic Face-Paint: This recipe works as well as the type that clowns use! Mix two parts cornstarch with one part white vegetable shortening to make a non-toxic grease paint. Add a few drops of food coloring to create an assortment of colors.

 Never-Fail Finger Paint: Combine ¼ cup (60 mL) cornstarch with 2 cups (500 mL) water. Boil the cornstarch mixture on the stove until it reaches the consistency of paint. Remove from the stove and pour into separate dishes. Create different colors by adding a few drops of food coloring to each dish; mix well until the desired color is achieved. Cornstarch finger paint is non-toxic and edible.

 Inexpensive Body Powder Recipe: Put 2 drops perfume into a sealable bag with 2 cups (500 mL) cornstarch. Shake and apply to face or body.

- Little Bobby just learned how to tie his shoes and the knots are impossible to undo. Stay calm and sprinkle a little cornstarch onto the laces to help work out the knots.

- When making gravy there are advantages to using cornstarch rather than flour. Cornstarch has twice the "thickening power" of flour (you only need to use half as much). If a recipe calls for ¼ cup (60 mL) flour, use just 2 tbsp. (30 mL) cornstarch. Cornstarch thickens with a satiny smoothness and glossy appearance. It adds no taste to mask the flavor of foods. Use 1 tbsp. (15 mL) cornstarch to thicken every 2 cups (500 mL) of liquid to a medium consistency. Cornstarch is mixed with a little cold liquid and is stirred into hot food during the final stage of cooking. It must be cooked to 203°F (95°C) before thickening begins. At that point, it will quickly thicken and the sauce turns from opaque to transparent (sauces will thin if cooked too long, boiled or vigorously stirred). **Tip**: If problems occur when using cornstarch, the best remedy is to add more liquid instead of additional cornstarch. In many cases, there may not be enough liquid to begin with, which does not allow the starch granules to enlarge to full capacity.

- Pour a small amount of cornstarch into a bag of stuck-together marshmallows and shake the bag so that the cornstarch coats the marshmallows. Gently pull apart marshmallows, once coated they will no longer be sticky. **Note**: Icing sugar can be used in the same way.

Household Superstar ... Mayonnaise

"I can still remember the warm freshly filled jars of mayonnaise, cooling on the kitchen counter. Egg salad sandwiches, tomato sandwiches, mayonnaise sandwiches – you name it, I'd make an excuse to eat them, I was 12. I hadn't heard of cholesterol or weight gain. Mom hadn't heard of Miracle Whip. Sadly, as soon as she did, she stopped making mayonnaise." *Janet Stewart, CBC News at 6*

White heat marks and water rings on wood furniture are unsightly but often simple to remove. Rub mayonnaise onto the stain, allow to sit for a few hours, then wipe with a dry towel. (from *Household Solutions 1 with Substitutions.*)

- Mayonnaise deteriorates quickly in warm weather. Put mayonnaise in potato salad after you arrive at a potluck gathering, just before serving.

- Freezing of mayonnaise is not recommended because it will separate. However, some cooks have successfully re-emulsified frozen mayonnaise with the whirl of the blender.

Remove tree sap from hands by working mayonnaise onto skin; then rinse.

Use mayonnaise to condition your hair! Cover your head with mayonnaise, pop on a shower cap, wait several minutes and shampoo. The mayonnaise will moisturize your hair and give it a lustrous sheen.

Need a facial? Use mayonnaise. Apply and leave for 20 minutes before you wash your face. It firms and smoothes and also works great around the eyes!

Over-the-counter lice shampoos are pesticides and may cause harm to children with lice as well as to the individual applying the product. In addition to being toxic, lice shampoos have not been 100% effective in killing lice. Alternative treatments such as petroleum jelly, olive oil and mayonnaise are effective, cost less and are not harmful to your child. **Note**: Mayonnaise is often the treatment of choice because it smothers live lice. Rub scalp with lots of mayonnaise. Wrap head with plastic (except when treating children). Leave for 4-6 hours (there's an attractive image). Wash out with a biodegradable dish soap or baby shampoo. **Additional Tip**: To prevent lice from making their home on your scalp, shampoo with neem shampoo. *Submitted by Wendy Sidloski*

DID YOU KNOW? In January 2007, Egyptian researchers completed an experiment about the effectiveness of neem shampoo (a botanical shampoo made from properties of the evergreen neem tree found in India, neem oil has been used for centuries in the treatment of skin disorders) on killing lice. In the experiment, 60 children – all heavily infested with head lice – were treated with neem shampoo. The study showed that if the hair was washed with 4-6 tsp. (20-30 mL) of neem shampoo, then left in hair for at least 10 minutes, it is highly effective against all stages of head lice.

Professional florists use this trick, to keep houseplant leaves shiny and clean; rub a little mayonnaise on leaves with a paper towel and they will stay bright and shiny for weeks, even months, at a time.

Mayonnaise removes scuff marks. Just smear on and wipe off.

- Use mayonnaise to remove ballpoint ink marks from hands. Works in a jiffy!

To shine your shoes in a hurry, spread mayonnaise on a coffee filter and wipe over shoes.

- To give roast chicken a beautiful golden brown texture, rub mayonnaise over the chicken and place it in the oven for the required time. For extra crispness, uncover the pan for the last half hour.

- When your mayonnaise jar is almost empty and you just can't get that last little bit, sprinkle a few drops of vinegar inside, add flavorful herbs and shake well. You'll have enough salad dressing for one salad.

Remove dead skin by dabbing chapped area with mayonnaise; leave it to dry for a few minutes. Rub the area with damp fingers and dead skin will disappear from feet, knees, elbows, or face.

Homemade Mayonnaise: Place 3 egg yolks in a mixing bowl. Add 2 tbsp. (30 mL) white vinegar, 2 tbsp. (30 mL) water and 2 tbsp. (30 mL) lemon juice. Heat the contents in a double boiler until 150°F (66°C) as this reduces the risk of food poisoning. Stir constantly. Remove from heat and cool to room temperature. Add 2 tsp. (10 mL) dry mustard, ½ tsp. (2 mL) salt, ½ tsp. (2 mL) pepper. Add any of the following: fresh garlic, Dijon mustard or curry powder. Very slowly add 1 cup (250 mL) extra virgin olive oil. Add more oil as needed until you reach the proper consistency. **Note:** This isn't a low-fat product, so use sparingly if cutting calories. However, this recipe does call for heart healthy oil.

- **Additional Notes**: Store homemade mayonnaise sealed in the refrigerator for up to three days. If homemade mayonnaise does not bond, add ¼ tsp. (1 mL) commercial mayonnaise.

WARNING: Pregnant women are advised not to eat homemade mayonnaise due to the raw eggs in the recipe.

Solutions 3

Household Superstar ... Tea Tree Oil

Tea tree oil, also known as Melaleuca, has been around for thousands of years and was used as a general antiseptic by the aborigine tribes who were known to chew on the leaves. It was used as a medicinal agent for cuts, burns, bites and many skin ailments. Tea tree oil contains a complex of over 100 naturally occurring compounds and is a clear and colorless to pale yellow liquid with a distinct odor. A broad range of cosmetic, dental, veterinary, industrial and household industries make use of tea tree oil on a daily basis. The key to tea tree oil's medicinal effectiveness are two chemical constituents found in the oil: cineole and terpinen. Although both are bactericidal and germicidal, cineole can be a powerful skin irritant. Therefore, tea tree oils with low cineole and high terpinen contents are preferred.

 The scent of tea tree oil may not be for everyone but those who enjoy it can use it for aromatherapy purposes. A few drops in a diffuser or even just on a cotton ball can allow the essential oil fragrance to be released into the air as a non-toxic air freshener.

- Tea tree oil benefits require proper storage. Tea tree oil is remarkably stable if protected from prolonged exposure to high temperatures and especially from the damaging effects of light. Thus, tea tree oil must be packaged in protective amber glass bottles or opaque containers. Tea tree oil is available at most health food stores and many grocery stores.

 Repel Bugs with Tea Tree Oil: In a spray bottle mix 15 drops of tea tree oil and 1 gallon (4.5 L) water. Spray solution where ants tend to enter the home. On that note, wipe cupboards out with the same solution to keep cockroaches away.

- Got bedbugs? Make a solution of tea tree oil and water; generously spray the mattress to zap each and every one of them. If bedbugs get out of hand call a professional.

- Get rid of ticks with tea tree oil. Hold a cotton swab with tea tree oil onto the tick and wait 30 seconds until the tick lets go, flush tick down the toilet. Great results!

Athlete's foot is commonly associated with a fungal nail infection and should be treated by a physician. Consider discussing tea tree oil as a remedy with your doctor. Treat the affected area twice per day and for a few days after the symptoms disappear in order to prevent recurrence.

Mold Killer in the Bathroom: In a spray bottle, combine 2 tsp. (10 mL) tea tree oil and 2 cups (500 mL) water. Shake to blend. Spray on mold and the smell will dissipate.

Clean out dishwasher and hoses by adding 10 drops of tea tree oil to dishwasher dispenser, then fill with dishwasher detergent.

Freshen and disinfect your humidifier by adding 5 drops of tea tree oil to the machine.

All-Purpose Cleaner: Add 1 tsp. (5 mL) tea tree oil to 2 gallons (9 L) when washing windows, floors, toilets, bathrooms and kitchen surfaces.

Shower curtains stay mildew free if soaked in tea tree oil and water before washing. Add a few drops of tea tree oil to rinse water.

Prevent soap scum on shower doors by wiping them with a solution of tea tree oil and water.

For diaper washing, add 20 drops tea tree oil to approximately 1 gallon (4.5 L) of water and stir. Soak diapers overnight before washing.

Remove scuff marks from a vinyl or linoleum floor by rubbing with a damp cloth and a few drops of tea tree oil.

Add a cotton ball with a few drops of tea tree oil into your vacuum cleaner bag to freshen rooms and kill dust mites as you clean.

Put a cotton ball with a few drops of oil on it into your leather shoes/boots when you store them to prevent mildew growth.

Use tea tree oil on a cloth to remove tar from feet.

Chewing gum can be removed from hair or clothing with an application of tea tree oil.

Note: Use tea tree oil with caution. Animals and humans have been poisoned from accidental ingestion of tea tree oil.

Solutions 3

Household Superstar ... Toothpaste

Long ago, people did not use toothpaste to clean their pearly whites. Instead they used ground-up chalk or charcoal or lemon juice or ashes or tobacco and honey mixed together. Since that time toothpaste has evolved from a smile maker to a versatile cleaning product.

- Toothpaste can be used to clean the plate of a household iron which tends to become stained with melted fabric, watermarks and calcium deposits. Rub toothpaste onto the plate of an iron when it is cool. Leave for 5 minutes and wipe. Before applying the iron to fine fabrics, heat the iron as normal and rub it over a scrap of cloth.

- When toothpaste hardens and sticks to the bathroom sink apply cooking oil to the affected areas; it will loosen the sticky mess. Wipe and apply dish soap to remove the oily residue.

- You can use toothpaste to clean your bathroom sink – simply rub it around the bowl and rinse. This freshens the drain and prevents stale smells.

- Zap sticky tar on feet by rubbing them with non-gel toothpaste. Rinse.

- Do your hands reek from fish, onions or garlic? You bet they do! Wash your hands with toothpaste and they'll smell great.

- Toothpaste deodorizes bottles and jars carrying an ugly smell. It also works for sour milk in baby bottles or any type of drink that has sat for too long in a glass, mug or bottle. Fill the container with warm water. Add a dab of toothpaste, let sit for an hour and rinse.

- Sally ran in the doorway after receiving top marks at school and left scuff-marks on the floor, what should she do? Make her milk and cookies to praise her for her school marks and then hand her a tube of non-gel toothpaste and a green abrasive sponge so that she can clean up the scuffmarks. Apply non-gel, non-bleach toothpaste with a tissue, rub and wipe off (this also works to zap scuffmarks on shoes).

- Apply non-gel, non-bleach tooth-paste to stains such as ink and lipstick. Squeeze on the spot; scrub and rinse.

- Use regular toothpaste and a damp cloth to remove Kool-Aid and juice moustaches from children's mouths. Wipes off with little effort!

- Clean your nails by squeezing toothpaste onto an old toothbrush. Wet nails and brush them thoroughly.

- You can use toothpaste to hang posters on walls. **Caution**: Avoid using toothpaste for valuable posters; the ink may become damaged over time.

- Use an old toothbrush and non-gel, non-bleach toothpaste to clean costume jewelry. Rinse thoroughly.

- It can take children to reach age 6 before they learn to spit out toothpaste instead of eating it. If you choose to purchase commercial toothpastes, encourage children not to swallow toothpaste by purchasing adult flavors instead of yummy kid flavors. They both contain the same amount of fluoride.

- According to the Canadian Dental Association, "Regular exposure to slightly elevated amounts of fluorides, during the period of tooth formation from birth to approximately six years of age, is associated with dental fluorosis. This is characterized by white areas and occasionally brown stains, on the teeth." Think you are not getting enough fluoride? Remember that fluoride is found in air, water and soils. As well, vegetation and many foods contain at least trace amounts of fluorides. Foods that contain the highest levels of fluorides include fish, shellfish, meat and tea.

- Consider using an alternative to commercially sold toothpaste:

 Homemade Toothpaste Recipe #1: Combine, 2 tbsp. (30 mL) baking soda, ½ tsp. (2 mL) sea salt, 1 tsp. (5 mL) vodka, 2 drops of wintergreen and 2 drops of peppermint oil. Shake and use.

 Easy Toothpaste Recipe #2: Combine 1 tsp. (5 mL) baking soda and ¼ cup (60 mL) water. Swish and use.

 DID YOU KNOW?

The first recorded form of a toothbrush was burnt toast!

Solutions 3

Household Superstar ... Vodka

Vodka is a distilled spirit with a high alcohol content that can be produced from a number of different materials. Most vodka produced these days is made from grain, though some is still made from potatoes. Instead of drinking the stuff, why not get creative?

 Make your own waterless hand cleaner: Combine ¼ cup (60 mL) Aloe Vera gel, ¼ cup (60 mL) vodka and a few drops of essential oil (optional). Shake and store in a spray pump bottle. Makes 4 oz. (113 g).

 Take a bandage off of your skin with ease by soaking the sticky area with vodka. The vodka dissolves adhesive making it easier to remove the bandage.

 Soothe a jelly fish sting by dampening a cloth with vodka and blotting the affected area. The vodka will disinfect, clean and ease the pain.

 Clean your eyeglasses by pouring a few drops of vodka onto a soft cloth and gently wiping.

 Make a handy ice pack by pouring ½ cup (125 mL) vodka and ½ cup (125 mL) water into a sealable freezer bag. Freeze and apply to aches, pains or black eyes.

 Make your own mouthwash by mixing 1 tsp. (5 mL) powdered cinnamon with 1 cup (250 mL) vodka. Mix with warm water and rinse your mouth.

 To cure foot odor, wipe or soak feet in vodka.

 Easy Air Freshener Recipe: In a spray bottle combine ¼ cup (60 mL) vodka, ¼ cup (60 mL) distilled water and 20 drops essential oil. Spray room, mattress and furniture.

At the end of one of my presentations in Victoria, BC, a man named James Weir from Ontario shared with me that he was at a back stage tour of the Stratford Shakespearean Festival in Ontario. During the tour he was told that after each performance the costumes are sprayed with vodka to keep them smelling fresh.

Make Your Own Vanilla Extract for Baking: Combine 1 vanilla bean in a container of vodka. The biggest thing you need is time, because the mixture needs to sit for about 8 weeks to reach its full potential.

Feelings Nothin' More Than Feelings Body Oil: Combine ¼ cup (60 mL) vodka, ¼ cup (60 mL) water and 3 tbsp. (45 mL) sweet almond oil. Pour all ingredients into a spray pump bottle and close. Shake and use.

Shine Chrome, Glass and Porcelain: Soak a soft, clean cloth with vodka and polish bathroom fixtures.

Betsy left for her first date and the bathroom mirror was covered with hairspray. How did she clean the mirror when she returned? She made a solution of 50/50 vodka and water, (no, not to drink) and wiped the mirror with 3 day old or older newspaper.

Clean tiles in the bathroom by spraying with vodka. Leave for 5 minutes and rinse (great for getting rid of soap scum).

Sanitize kitchen countertops by spraying and scrubbing with vodka.

Whenever you cut "bulb" flowers like tulips or irises, mix together 3 cups (750 mL) of water and 1 tbsp. (15 mL) of vodka into a vase. The vodka will keep the stems of the flowers nice and firm so that you don't end up with slumped over blooms.

Use vodka to clean gold and gemstone jewelry. Soak your jewels in a dish of vodka and then wipe with a soft toothbrush. The vodka will dissolve grime and leave your bling, blingy.

Remove odors from wigs by spritzing them with 50/50 vodka and water. The alcohol smell evaporates quickly leaving a fresh smell behind.

The Seasons

Spring into Spring

Are you one of the 67% of North Americans who regularly spring cleans? If you are the type who likes to clean your home one room at a time, **the rule is: Don't leave until you are done that room.** Arm yourself with cleaning supplies, trash bags and "give away" boxes. Turn on your favorite music and have fun!

MAIN LIVING AREA

- Wash the walls. For stained areas, wash with bar soap and a green abrasive pad. Apply the soap to the wall and rinse with clear water. To clean rough textured walls, use old nylon stockings or socks rather than a sponge because they won't tear and leave difficult-to-remove bits on the surface. Spot clean doorknobs and light switches. Consider fresh paint.
- To really freshen up knickknacks wash them instead of just dusting them. Wash all curtains, blinds and other window coverings according to care directions. Wash and fluff throw pillows. Clean ceiling fans with a microfiber cloth.
- Steam clean all carpeting/area rugs and furniture. Also, replace furnace and air filters.
- Clean windows and screens. An alternative to washing screens with soap and water is to use a steam cleaner. Steam cleaners can be rented for a reasonable price and screens will look like new when the job is finished. You can also use a steam cleaner to clean the exhaust fan above your range to remove layers of cooking grime from the stovetop. However, Sunlight bar soap, although it may sound old-fashioned, is my number one choice for the job. Check out *Household Solutions 2*, page 11, for the great Squeaky Clean Window recipe.
- Vacuum and wash the lint trap on the dryer and wash the inside of the washing machine. Also vacuum out the area inside the dryer, underneath the catcher and inside the exhaust hose that runs from the back of the dryer and vents to the outside. A clogged hose will not only cut down on your dryer's efficiency and release unwanted moisture into the house (which can cause mold), it can also be a fire hazard.

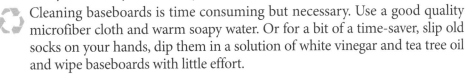

- Replace the batteries in your smoke detector and carbon monoxide detector twice a year (when the clocks change). Test all smoke and carbon-monoxide alarms at least monthly to ensure that they are operating properly. As well, check the pressure gauge on the fire extinguisher.
- Vacuum vents and behind large furniture. Move the couch, beds and other heavy furniture you normally don't mess with.
- Cleaning baseboards is time consuming but necessary. Use a good quality microfiber cloth and warm soapy water. Or for a bit of a time-saver, slip old socks on your hands, dip them in a solution of white vinegar and tea tree oil and wipe baseboards with little effort.

KITCHEN

- Deep clean the oven and stove tops. Clean out the refrigerator, freezer, pantry and cabinets. Did you know that you should clean the coils underneath the front panel of the refrigerator every 6 months to keep it running efficiently?
- Check your inventory of spices and condiments and restock.
- Wash the inside of the garbage can.

BATHROOM

- Check the condition of the towels, do laundry. Do any need to be replaced? Replace the toilet brush.
- Wash fabric shower curtains and bathroom rugs, replace shower liners. Clean shower doors and drains. Clean grout and tiles.
- Vacuum underneath the sink and in the drawers. Make sure that no mold is forming in hidden areas such as behind the toilet wall and tank.
- Wash the liquid soap container or soap dish. Replenish as needed.

Note: Keep cleaning products in their original containers with labels intact. It is important to know what the product name is; especially if a child accidentally swallows it.

Every year on April 22nd over 180 countries celebrate Earth Day. You can reduce your impact on the environment by reducing energy usage in the home. The average home uses most of its energy for heating; 46% of the average home's total energy consumption. Water heating accounts for 30%; running appliances, 17%; lighting, 6%; and space cooling is 1%.

Solutions 3

Get Organized

Know what "organized" looks and feels like? Organized spaces are simple to use. They make sense. Every item in your home has a location. Organized spaces feel calm, open and welcoming.

- Say so long to shoe racks. The next time you purchase a new pair of shoes don't throw the box out. Instead take a photo of the shoes and tape it to the outside of the box. You will no longer need to open each box to see what is inside and the boxes stack neatly on your shelf.

- Use a makeup bag or tackle box to get organized when you are on the go. Fill it with the following and store it in the trunk (use caution with small children): Tape, scissors, note pad, pen, mirror, empty cup, permanent marker, stapler, tape measure, paper clips, rubber bands, headache medicine, needle and thread, dental floss, breath spray, tweezers, safety pins, bandages, granola bars, comb, baby wipes or waterless hand cleaner, nail file, clippers and super glue. What have you got to lose?

- For manuals and warranties on all household appliances and electronics, store them in a 3" (8 cm) ringed binder filled with plastic, see-thru page protectors. It keeps them in order, all together and just like new.

- Calling all Pack Rats! If you have a hard time throwing things out, put the items in a box with a destroy date written onto it (about one year from the date). If you find yourself needing to go into it to find something and you end up actually using that item, keep it. Anything left in the box at the end of the year should be properly sorted.

- Many of us already use empty vitamin or prescription bottles to store nails. Now, for the next step, use packing tape to secure one nail to the front of the bottle. This way you will know which type of nail is inside the bottle.

- Remembering birthdays is one task, remembering to send a card before that date is another story. As you record a birthday on your calendar, make yourself a note a week or two before the actual birthday, reminding yourself to buy a gift or send an ECard.

- Ya gotta have a giveaway box. Toss in everything you find that is cluttering up your home and you want to get rid of. When the box is full, pop it into your trunk and immediately drop it off at a self-help store or place it in a designated area for your next yard sale.

- Get organized the night before work. Install a hook on the inside of your closet door and hang up clothing that is to be worn the next day. **Tip**: Hooks are inexpensive and great for hanging belts and neckties.

- To organize scarves, glue numerous clothespins to the door of a closet. Clip 2 or 3 scarves per clothespin; this will keep scarves visible and wrinkle-free.

To organize books (e.g. coloring books, paperbacks, magazines and catalogs), take empty cereal boxes and cut them to form the shape of a magazine holder or simply cut them to the desired height for children's books. Let children paint them, apply stickers, fabrics, buttons or paste on pictures cut from old magazines.

Use the empty roll from wrapping paper to store flags. Roll up the flag and slide it inside the roll. Make the roll clearly visible by labeling it with marker.

Use empty paper towel rolls to store plastic grocery bags, just keep stuffing bags into the tube (or empty tissue box) until it is full and then start on a new one. All of the tubes can be banded together with rubber bands and placed where you might need the bags. To store clear bags from the vegetable isle. Wrap one clear bag into a roll and then wrap each new bag around the first one and store in a drawer.

- Keep all of your jewelry in little boxes (or if you have a teenage daughter and she has more jewelry than you, pass this tip onto her). Open and lay boxes and lids in a dresser drawer, fill with jewelry. When she opens her dresser drawer she can see all of her jewelry at once and when she closes the drawer it keeps them safe and dust free. **Extra Tip**: Tired of fumbling in a jewelry box for a pair of earrings? Buy some heavy-duty screen at a hardware store. Frame a piece of screen in a pretty picture frame. Place your earrings and tack pins through the screen and fasten with the earring backs. *Submitted by Margret Malaviya*

- Keep jewelry safe by hiding it in a tennis ball with a slit cut into it.

- Wax paper taped inside slatted closet doors will help to keep out moths and dust.

 Green Idea: Don't throw away old eyeglasses. Whether they are broken or in great shape contact your local eyewear store or Lion's Club Recycle for Sight program. They will remake the glasses and send them to people who desperately require eyewear.

Solutions 3

Additional Organization Hints

- Men who travel on business will really enjoy this little tidbit. Keep your ties from wrinkling by laying the tie on one page of a magazine; bring the second end of the tie back down a few pages later. Then fold a few more pages over and bring the tie back up. Your ties will never again be wrinkled!

 Make your own yarn holder. Heat the black part of a 2 L pop bottle with a hair dryer and remove the ring. Cut the bottom part of the clear plastic container with a knife. Insert yarn inside the bottle and run the yarn through the top opening. Slip the ring back on the bottom end of the bottle. If the ring is too loose, tape it to the clear part of the bottle.

- **Better bedmaking**: To make a bed that looks tidy, stitch a thread in the center of all sheets and blankets. Line up threads with the center of the headboard to make a taut and tidy bed.

To store rolls of gift wrap, use an empty wine box. The dividers help hold the rolls upright in a relatively small space. You can store the box in the guest room closet or basement.

 If possible, use a **Blue Box** to recover any recyclable items you have around the house and place it curbside for collection on your scheduled recycling date.

Choose and Maintain a Solid Exterior in the Spring

The trouble with owning a home is that no matter where you sit, you're looking at something you should be doing.

- If efflorescence (white salt residue) is present on bricks scrub it with a brush. Do not use liquid cleaners or water because they will dissolve and soak into the brick.

- When brick is clean and dry, apply a sealer or paint the bricks using waterproof paint.

- To remedy paint stains on brick, spray the brick with a hose. Mix a solution of 2 lbs. (.90 kg) TSP (trisodium phosphate), or a strong detergent, apply, allow it to soak in and then scrub with a stiff nylon-bristle brush (don't use a wire brush). For resistant spots, repeat several times. If scrubbing with this solution doesn't work, try applying a water-based paint stripper (test on an inconspicuous area first).

- To replace a damaged brick, begin by putting on eye protection and heavy-duty gloves. Using a cold chisel and heavy hammer break apart the damaged brick. **Tip**: If you are removing several bricks, then start at the top and work down. As an alternative, use a power drill and masonry-cutting wheel to score the old bricks before cutting them out with a chisel. Be very careful not to damage surrounding bricks. Once the brick pieces are removed, chisel out any old mortar and clean the joints of any loose mortar with a brush and vacuum. Rinse the cleaned area.

- Stucco is a great material. If installed correctly, it will very likely last a long time. The key is to choose the material that suits your tastes. Make sure you install it so that water (which will invariably get behind the stucco) can get out before it damages the wood framing of your home.

- To give stucco a fresh look, clean it with a garden hose and sprayer filled with a very dilute solution of TSP (trisodium phosphate). Be sure to thoroughly rinse off the mixture.

- Fix very small cracks in stucco by filling them with a high-quality caulk, preferably one that can be painted over. Use your fingers to press it and a damp cloth to clean up excess.

- Deal with wider movement cracks by calling for professional repair that may include raking the cracks and filling them with a urethane sealant system or other treatment. Movement cracks and other serious problems, such as loose framing, cannot be cured by patches and paint.

- If you have vinyl siding, don't choose a dark paint color. Dark colors absorb more heat from the sun and can cause vinyl siding panels to buckle.

- Relatively new exterior finishes include brick and stone veneer. This includes thin bricks or stones and cultured synthetic masonry materials (½-4"/1.25-10 cm thick). These products are very durable, fire-proof and solid. Hose off annually. The disadvantage is installation is costly.

- Be careful when choosing siding. Many inexpensive brands do not offer enough pure vinyl to prevent cracking or lack the key elements needed to prevent fading. A high quality vinyl siding offers a superior underlay system and resists peeling, cracking, waving, fading and high winds. When quality siding starts looking dull, just clean it with a little soap and water to restore it to like new condition.

- Protect wood siding with paint, stain or 2 coats of water repellent preservatives. Reapply every 3 years. **Tip 1**: When water stops beading and rolling off the wall, it is time for a fresh coat. **Tip 2**: Use rust resistant screws on warped boards to hold them against the house.

- When painting windows, apply wet newspapers on the glass to guard against splashing. You can splatter all you want and, better yet, when you remove the newspaper, there's no sticky residue to clean.

Green Energy Saving Tips for Doors and Windows

Caulk and weather strip your home to seal air leaks around movable joints, such as windows or doors. To determine how much weather stripping you will need, add the perimeters of all windows and doors to be weather stripped, then add 5-10% to accommodate for waste. Also, consider that weather stripping comes in varying depths and widths.

Seal electrical outlets and switches on outside walls with foam gaskets; on inside walls use childproof plugs or combination cover plates.

Keep window curtains open during the day in winter. This allows passive solar energy into your home and can save you up to 5% on home heating. Close the curtains in the evening.

Install energy-efficient windows and doors and only purchase windows and doors that have been properly certified.

Install storm windows. If your windows are single-glazed, they will add an extra layer of protection. Windows can account for up to 25% of total house heat loss.

Replace exterior doors that are in poor condition with core-insulated, steel-clad doors or storm doors.

Insulate basement windows with a piece of 3" (8 cm) Styrofoam inserted between the inside window and the storm window.

An old shower curtain gives added insulation to drafty windows, especially in the basement, if you hang it up behind the curtains.

Don't heat your closet – keep the door closed. Also, keep doors closed to rooms that are not being used.

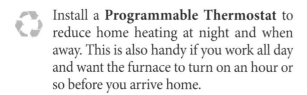

Install a **Programmable Thermostat** to reduce home heating at night and when away. This is also handy if you work all day and want the furnace to turn on an hour or so before you arrive home.

Big Ideas for Small People in the Summertime

If you have kids at your house, you will inevitably want them to go outside. That's right, turn off the TV and play! Here are tips and recipes that will make summer exciting and safe.

- Before using a sandbox, rub talcum powder on exposed skin; it will make brushing off any sand much easier when your kids are ready to come indoors. After outdoor sand play, use a soft brush to remove any sand particles from children's clothes before they return inside. Keep a mat by the door to reduce the amount of sand that is tracked indoors.

- **Cleaning Your Trampoline**: Use a large broom to sweep (or shop vac.) any loose debris off the mat. Wash the trampoline mat with warm water and dish soap. Scrub the mat with brushes or sponges. Rinse all soap off so that the mat does not become slimy. Leave the mat to air dry.

- Outdoor activities often include bike riding. Wear a bicycle helmet, it should not be optional, for anyone in your family, no matter where you are or how short the ride. In many areas it's the law. Here's why: Most bike accidents involve a head injury, so a crash could mean permanent brain damage or death for someone who doesn't wear one while riding. In fact, each year in the US, about half a million kids are seriously injured in bicycle-related accidents and most could have been avoided if a helmet was worn.

- Be sure to replace any helmet made before 1999. If your child hits the surface hard while wearing a helmet, replace it. Helmets lose their capacity to absorb shock after taking serious hits. A few bike helmets can be used as protection for other activities, but in general, they're best suited to biking. Most helmets are made for one specific type of activity: for example, special helmets are made for in-line skating, baseball and snowmobiling. Kids should not wear any helmet when they're on a playground or climbing a tree; there is a risk of strangulation from the chin strap during these types of activities.

- In addition to wearing a helmet, children should be dressed in light or bright colored clothing to help them stand out while riding their bikes. Avoid riding in low light conditions or at night when it is tough for a motorist to see your child on their bike. Many parents have purchased reflective stripes for their kids coats that help them stand out while they are riding or walking.

 Sidewalk Chalk Recipe: In an empty margarine container, measure 2 parts plaster of Paris and slowly stir in 1 part water (or just a little less). Add coloring, either powdered or liquid tempera paint, food coloring, or acrylic craft paint. Mix and set aside to thicken. Add more water, if required, until it is the consistency of thick frosting, pour into small plastic molds. This is a fun activity for a child's birthday!

Homemade Sidewalk Chalk Molds: Use paper towel rolls (cut to desired length and covered on one end with plastic wrap, foil, duct tape or something similar), muffin or cupcake pans, Dixie cups, cookie cutters, small sand molds, soap molds, ice cube trays, clean prescription pill bottles or Popsicle molds. Line tubular molds such as Popsicle containers with waxed paper before filling with the dried chalk (see above recipe) should slide out easily. It may take several days for your homemade chalk to harden.

Caution: Making chalk is a messy business; cover your work surface with newspaper before you begin.

Important: Avoid breathing in the dust of plaster of Paris and follow all safety precautions written on the box.

Best Bubble Making Solution: In a bucket combine: 1 cup (250 mL) water, 2 tbsp. (30 mL) glycerin (helps bubbles last longer) and 4 tbsp. (60 mL) biodegradable dish soap. Make the solution the day before you plan on using to increase bubble making capacity. Soft water is good for bubbles. Hard well water and any water containing high levels of iron are bad for bubbles. Remember, you don't want foam, it is the enemy of bubbles and will make your solution weaker. When you mix, don't stir too much. If foam forms, simply scoop it out. **Note**: wind and humidity can affect your solution enormously; for best results use solution early in the morning or evening (after rain is superb).

- **Homemade Bubble Wands**: A fly swatter will produce plenty of itty-bitty bubbles and cookie cutters and pipe cleaners are ideal for constructing bubble blowers. Twist two together into a circle and wind on another for a handle. Help your little ones bend the wire into shapes like hearts, diamonds or even stars. Of course, there's always the durable yet pliable wire clothes hanger. Unwind the hanger and straighten out the wire, loop a small section at one end and use the length as a handle.

Yummy-in-your-Tummy Homemade Ice Cream: In a pint-sized freezer bag, combine ½ cup (125 mL) whipping cream (unwhipped), 1 tbsp. (15 mL) sugar and ¼ tsp. (1 mL) vanilla (optional); zip shut. Place that bag into a quart-size or larger freezer bag. Add ice to the larger bag until half full and 6 tbsp. (90 mL) course salt. Zip shut. With oven mitts on; shake, turn, toss and mix the bag. In about 5-10 minutes, you will have cold hands and yummy ice cream! **Note**: Do not try to double this recipe, it doesn't work. Also, be sure to get all of the salt off of the smaller bag before opening.

Solutions 3

Caring for Patio Furniture

Before buying new patio furniture consider turning other items such as big empty spools that hold wires from construction sites into furniture. Make benches out of found wood: large logs turned on end make good stools and seats for your deck or patio.

- If you do shop for new patio furniture check warranties, care instructions and necessary maintenance of materials. Be sure the furniture you choose is durable and that parts will be available when you need them.

- **Teak** will last a lifetime. The hardwood, Teak tree is native to Southeast Asia and Africa and grows to be 100' (30 m) tall. The only maintenance necessary for teak furniture is periodic cleaning with a soft bristle brush, then rinse the entire piece to remove dirt and any remaining solution. For deeper cleaning and tackling stains use a teak cleaner. This will remove the silver-gray patina and restore the furniture's original color. **Tip:** For extra protection apply a teak sealer.

- **Cedar** wood is naturally resistant to weather and over time changes to a silvery gray weathered look that many people prefer. Unfinished Northern White or Western Red Cedar can be cleaned using a solution of 2 cups (500 mL) vinegar to 10 cups (2.5 L) water and ¼ cup (60 mL) liquid detergent. Scrub with a soft brush. Other choices for wood furniture are: Cypress wood (resists insects and rot), Brazilian hardwood (heavy and durable) and Pine (resists weather, decay and insects).

- Cedar may be stained, painted or left as is; there are a variety of stains suitable for finishing cedar patio furniture. Choose a deep penetrating stain in order to preserve the wood and retain its natural beauty. The stain should have mildew inhibitors and water repellent additives. All penetrating stains go deep into the wood but do not form a surface barrier, this eliminates blistering and peeling (these stains are perfect for woods that have knots and coarse grain). All of these factors make stain preferable over paint. Follow manufacturer's instruction for application. Reapply every 2 to 3 years.

- If choosing to paint outdoor cedar furniture remember that all exterior paints will flake and peel over time. When this happens, scrape and apply new paint every other year in order to keep cedar furniture looking beautiful. Always follow the manufacturer's direction when applying exterior paint.

- Tɪᴘ 1: Avoid using oil-based exterior paint on cedar patio furniture because it attracts dust and dirt.

- Tɪᴘ 2: For regular cleaning of finished cedar patio furniture, wipe with a damp cloth.

- **Cast aluminum** makes a great choice for patio furniture. It is lightweight and resists rust. Also, cast aluminum can be as beautiful as other patio furniture constructed from different materials and it is simpler to care for and maintain. Clean with soap and water.

- If the paint on aluminum furniture is in poor condition, rub it gently with a piece of fine sandpaper to smooth it out. Use carwash polish to buff the furniture back to its original luster.

- If the finish of **wicker furniture** becomes damaged, bring it back to life by using a permanent marker, nail polish or touch-up paint that matches the color and blends away the exposed areas. To give wicker a whole new look, spray paint each piece with a can of outdoor spray paint (use a spray paint formulated for outdoor wood and wicker). Apply several coats on all sides of the furniture.

- All natural wickers tend to dry out if left in the sun. Therefore, keep natural wicker outdoor furniture in shady areas such as under trees, umbrellas, or on a shady side of the house.

- If you choose to completely repaint your **wrought iron** patio furniture, use a paint that is specially formulated for metal. Be sure to rough up the metal with sandpaper so that the paint adheres.

- If wrought iron becomes stained, sand with a light sand paper and apply touch-up paint. Apply thin coats of paint and allow paint to dry between coats.

- **Plastic** patio furniture is maintenance free and lightweight. To maintain, hose and vinyl clean with dish soap and water. Plastic furniture is great for the family on a budget. Modern plastic furniture is made to look like real wood without the hassle of stain and paint.

- When positioning patio furniture, allow at least 1' (50 cm) of floor space around each piece to avoid a crowded look and 2' (61 cm) for traffic flow paths.

- For the winter months, cover all patio furniture preferably in your garage or basement.

 If you're refinishing furniture or involved in an type of messy project, protect your clothes with an apron made from an old shower curtain.

 Use old shower curtains as a picnic tablecloth or as a drop sheet when painting or sanding.

Solutions 3

Preparing Garden Soil

Every gardener dreams of a garden bursting with yummy vegetables and oodles of pest-free plants. Reduce your workload by planning ahead and then watering and feeding when necessary to make the dream a reality.

- When creating a new garden spend a few days breaking up heavy soil to a depth of at least 18" (46 cm). If the soil is like clay, it will need compost or peat moss (two thirds) and sand (one third) to become a crumbly consistency, able to hold water. **Note:** Wear a mask and gloves when working with peat moss.

- When soil is crumbly, add compost or manure. There are a variety of manures to choose from: sheep, cow, chicken, mushroom, cottonseed meal, kelp meal, leather meal and worm castings, as well as synthetic fertilizers.

- All manures should be composted before being used on the vegetable garden. It is best to add the manure in the fall, after harvest, or in the spring, before planting. Put down a layer of 1-2" (2.5-5 cm) of manure; work it into the top 6-9" (15-23 cm) of soil.

- Test soil. Have you ever been disappointed with the performance of your vegetables or flowers, even though you gave them the best care you could? The pH level may be the problem. Test soil at home using a do-it-yourself kit or with a portable soil probe/pH meter. Or send a sample to a lab for a more in-depth analysis.

- Soil can be brought back to the ideal pH range of 6.5-7.0. You can make adjustments by applying soil amendments such as dolomite limestone or gypsum. The best way to make pH adjustments is to incorporate compost and mulch. Adjust pH gradually, over several seasons.

- Healthy soil with plenty of organic matter promotes healthy plant growth. One of the best sources of organic matter is Canadian sphagnum peat moss, which is a natural, organic soil conditioner. Its unique cell structure helps regulate moisture and air around plant roots, adds body to sandy soil and reduces runoff of nutrients present in or added to the soil.

- The next time you spread grass seed, mix the seed with ordinary white flour. That way you will be able to see which areas you missed.

- Good drainage is important for healthy soil. Soggy soil prevents root growth and nutrient absorption by the plants. If soil drains too quickly, nutrients will leach out and plants will require more frequent watering. Test soil by digging a hole 6" (15 cm) across by 1' (30 cm) deep; fill the hole with water and let drain; fill it again. Time how long it takes for the water to drain. If it takes more than 8 hours, drainage is a problem and will affect plant growth. To determine if the soil drains too quickly, water a small portion of the garden. Check the area after two days by digging a hole 6" (15 cm) deep. If the soil is dry to the bottom of the hole, it drains too quickly to promote good plant growth.

- Nitrogen increases green growth of plants. You need to increase nitrogen if older leaves are yellow and spindly at the bottom of the plant and the remaining foliage is light green. To increase nitrogen, add grass clippings and green vegetables, blood meal, cottonseed meal, alfalfa meal, fishmeal or fish emulsion.

- Phosphorus stimulates root growth and promotes seed and fruit maturation. Your plants are lacking phosphorus if the leaves have brittle roots, skinny stems and late fruit. Increase phosphorus to plants by adding bone meal to the garden.

- Potassium is helpful at reducing plant disease. If you notice irregular yellowing of low growing leaves and poor root growth, consider adding grass clippings, sulphate of potash and wood ashes.

- Calcium is important for root and leaf development. If you notice deformed leaves, weak stems and roots, add gypsum as this will lower alkalinity in the soil.

- All vegetables need some sunlight. The garden should receive at least 6 hours of direct sunlight each day (8 to 10 hours each day is ideal). Vegetables should therefore be planted away from the shade of buildings, trees and shrubs. Some leafy vegetables such as broccoli, spinach and lettuce tolerate shadier conditions than other vegetables; if the garden does not receive at least 6 hours of sunlight daily, consider a new location.

- Do not plant related vegetables in the same location in the garden more often than once in 3 years. Rotation prevents the build-up of insects and disease. Keep garden plans from previous years as a guide for rotating crops. Rotate crops.

- Sow some seeds directly in the ground as they grow best that way: beans, beets, carrots, chard, corn, lettuce, melons, peas, pumpkins, squash and turnips. Starting seeds is much less expensive than planting seedlings.

- Overwatering is the number one cause of death in most landscape plants. The surface of the soil should feel dry to the touch before adding water.

Solutions 3

Composting – It just doesn't get any Greener

○ Don't throw the contents from your vacuum cleaner in the garbage, add it to your compost pile. Most of the contents are made up of organic materials such as hair and dust particles (except for Lego pieces, which have a habit of disappearing).

○ The size of a compost pile, should be at least 1 cubic meter. If smaller, turn the pile more frequently or mix in more material.

○ The fastest way to make compost is to use the turnover method. It's also a little more work. Start in the fall and add the old leaves and grass clippings. Wait till spring. Add materials from the spring clean-up. Turn. If it's dry, add water. If the pile heats up and you add more kitchen wastes, turn about once a week to make sure oxygen is supplied to the center of the pile where it's hottest. It's ready when it is dark in color, emits an earthy smell and doesn't heat up even though there's enough moisture and air.

○ Use the layering method, if you're not in any hurry to see the end result. It's sort of the couch potato version of composting. In the fall, add your leaves, lawn rakings, garden material and kitchen scraps until the pile is 5-6" (12-16 cm) high. Hose it down with water. At this point, some composters add organic fertilizer: 2½ cups (625 mL) per square meter is recommended. Cover with 2" (5 cm) of stone- and stick-free soil. Continue layering the materials through the fall, winter and spring. If your pile is layered properly, there shouldn't be any smell.

○ Make your own liquid plant food by brewing small bags full of compost material and water.

○ Good compost ingredients are autumn leaves; coffee grounds; egg shells; grass clippings; plants and plant trimmings; shredded, ink-free paper; vegetable scraps. Do not compost bones, diseased plant material, grease, invasive plants or weeds with root systems or seeds (weeds in flower are okay to use), lawn clippings that have been chemically sprayed, meat and pet waste.

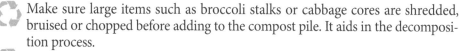

Make sure large items such as broccoli stalks or cabbage cores are shredded, bruised or chopped before adding to the compost pile. It aids in the decomposition process.

Cover food scraps with soil or other carbon-rich materials.

Composting does require some scientific know-how. It's called nitrogen/carbon ratio. The ratio refers to the balance of nitrogen and carbon in organic material. You will need roughly equal amounts of both, so when you add a pail of kitchen and plants scraps, be sure to throw in a pail full of leaves or dry grass clippings. Old leaves, dead grass from spring yard cleaning and small twigs add the carbon, which helps to prevent rotting; kitchen wastes add nitrogen, which helps speed up the composting process. If the pile smells, it means there's too much nitrogen. Just add more carbon to get rid of the odor.

Living in an apartment doesn't mean you can't have a compost pile. Shred kitchen waste into a black plastic bag, add a few cups of topsoil and close. Leave the bag in the sun – a patio or balcony will do. When the bag is full, the compost should take 3-4 weeks before it's ready to use. This compost is ideal for house plants or building flower beds.

Or consider The Worm Factory Vermicomposting System, an odorless bin that can be used indoors or out. It is constructed from recycled material. Check out www.vermiculture.ca/store/index. These compact, composters may also be available at your nearest health food store.

For those who don't compost, save vegetables and organic scraps and give them to those who do.

Solutions 3

Green Tips for Companions That Will Keep Your Garden Flourishing

Companion planting is based on the idea that certain plants can benefit others when planted in near proximity. Companion planting is an organic way to deter pests where limited or no pesticides or herbicides are used.

- **Basil**: Best friends are pepper, tomato and marigold. **Tip**: Plant seeds in rows 2' (60 cm) apart, spacing them ½" (1.25 cm) apart in the row. Most varieties grow to about 2' (60 cm). Pinch stems frequently to encourage basil to grow bushy and full.

- **Beans**: Best friends are celery and cucumbers. Enemies are onions and fennel. **Tip**: Beans grow best when the garden soil is well fertilized. For an area that is 10' (3 m) long and 10' (3 m) wide, use 2 to 3 lbs. (1 to 1.4 kg) of fertilizer such as 10-20-10. Spread the fertilizer evenly over the area. Then mix it in with the top 3-4" (8-10 cm) of soil.

- **Beets**: Best friends are bush beans, lettuce, onions, kohlrabi and most members of the cabbage family. Enemies are pole beans and mustard.

- **Carrots**: Best friends are leaf lettuce, radish, onions and tomatoes, carrots and parsley. Basil improves growth and flavor. Enemies are dill, cabbage and cauliflower. **Tip**: Carrot seed takes up to 10 days to germinate, you can throw in a bit of radish seed as a row marker until germination. Put in one seed every 8" (20 cm). Quick germinating radishes provide a convenient row marker and reminder as well as a tasty snack later on.

- **Corn**: Best friends are bush beans, pole beans, cucumber, melons, peas, squash, pumpkins and potatoes. It's enemy is the tomato. **Tip**: Plant your seeds 1" (2.5 cm) deep, in well-composted soil and spread the seeds thicker than suggested; perhaps 2 or 3" (5 or 8 cm) apart. Then thin them, if necessary, when they are a 3-4" (8-10 cm) high, to 1' (.30 m) apart.

- **Cucumbers**: Best friends are bush beans, pole beans, cabbage family, corn, dill, eggplant, lettuce, marigold, nasturtium, onions, peas, radish, tomato, savory and sunflower. Enemies are strong herbs and potatoes.

- Cucumbers grow in a vine-like fashion so feel free to plant them near a trellis for a beautiful background.

- **Garlic**: Helps keep aphids away from roses. Accumulates sulphur, a naturally occurring fungicide that will help in the garden with disease prevention. Garlic offends moths, Japanese beetles, root maggots, snails and carrot root fly. Researchers have observed that time-released garlic capsules planted at the bases of fruit trees actually keep deer away, worth a try! Concentrated garlic sprays have been observed to repel and kill whiteflies, aphids, mosquitoes and fungus gnats among others with as little as a 6-8% concentration! It is safe for use on orchids too.

- **Lettuce**: Best friends are bush beans, pole beans, carrots, cucumbers, onion, radish and strawberries. **Tip**: Lettuce is best when it is grown quickly and pampered a bit with good soil and adequate moisture so it doesn't bolt (send up a flowering stalk) or become bitter and tough.

- **Onions**: Best friends are lettuce, beetroot, strawberries and tomatoes. Enemies are peas and beans. **Tip**: When planting onions, make sure to have your soil prepared first. Clear out debris and rocks and mix in a fertilizer rich with phosphorus.

- **Peas**: Best friend is beans. Enemies are onions, chives and garlic. **Tip**: Select a location in full sun and provide support in the form of a trellis or unused tomato cage. Do not grow peas in the same spot more than once every five years.

- **Potatoes**: Best friends are beans, corn, cabbage, peas and eggplant. Enemies are cucumber, pumpkin, squash and sunflower. **Tip**: Plant Lamium nearby, not too close though as they can be invasive, but they will repel potato bugs, a big problem for many gardeners!

- **Radish**: Best friends are bush beans, pole beans, carrots, cucumber, lettuce, melons, peas and squash. Enemy is Hyssop. **Tip**: Radish grows best in the spring and autumn and will tolerate light winter frosts. It requires full to partial sun, ample water and rich, fast draining soil.

- **Spinach**: Best friends are celery, eggplant and cauliflower. **Tip**: To speed germination, soak seeds for 15-20 minutes in compost tea.

 Extra Hint: Bend the tops of potato plant stems so that nutrients are forced to the bottom of each plant. This provides a better potato yield. *Submitted by Julie Parisloff*

- **Strawberry**: Best friends are bush beans, lettuce, onion and spinach. Enemy is cabbage. **Tip**: Once you've got berries growing in and filling out, pick them about every other day. Save bruised berries for jams and jellies by separating them when harvesting. Pick out all the ripe berries, not just the large ones that look tempting. You'll want more berries later and picking more now will mean more in the future.

- **Tomato**: Best friends are asparagus, basil, bean, cabbage family, carrots, celery, chive, cucumber, garlic, head lettuce, marigold, mint, nasturtium, onion, parsley and pepper. Enemies are pole beans, corn, dill, fennel and potato. **Tip**: Bury tomato plants deeper than they come in the pot, all the way up to a few top leaves. Pinch off the bottom leaves of your seedling. Tomato plants develop roots along the stem and should be set deeply with the first set of leaves near the soil surface.

 Chamomile: Deters flies and mosquitoes and gives strength to any plant growing nearby.

Marigolds: (Calendula): Given a lot of credit as a pest deterrent. Keeps soil free of bad nematodes and discourages insects. Plant freely throughout the garden. The marigolds you choose must be a scented variety for them to work. **Note**: Marigolds do attract spider mites and slugs.

Peppers: Like high humidity, which can be helped along by planting with some kind of dense-leaf or ground cover companion, e.g., marjoram and basil. They also need direct sunlight but their fruit can be harmed by it. Pepper plants grown together, or with tomatoes, can shelter the fruit from sunlight and raise the humidity level.

DID YOU KNOW?

Honey Bees pollinate much of what we eat – such as blueberries apples, berries, cherries, melons, grapefruit, avocados, squash, broccoli, carrots, onions, etc. 80% of our food depends on the pollination of honey bees. Sadly, millions of honeybees are suddenly dying off. Gardeners can make a positive difference by creating pollinator-friendly gardens by growing native plants and eliminating pesticide use; plant flowers that bloom for the entire season.

Green Solutions for Gorgeous Pest Reduced Gardens

"We can complain because rose bushes have thorns, or rejoice because thorn bushes have roses." *Abraham Lincoln*

Not yielding apples from your apple tree? Prune the tree each year in early spring to get it going.

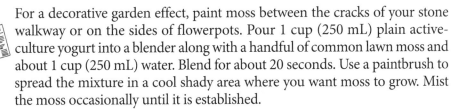

For a decorative garden effect, paint moss between the cracks of your stone walkway or on the sides of flowerpots. Pour 1 cup (250 mL) plain active-culture yogurt into a blender along with a handful of common lawn moss and about 1 cup (250 mL) water. Blend for about 20 seconds. Use a paintbrush to spread the mixture in a cool shady area where you want moss to grow. Mist the moss occasionally until it is established.

If outdoor plants start to look unhealthy and you notice small lumps on the roots, your garden may have a nematode infection. These are tiny worms that invade the root especially in tuberous plants like carrots and potatoes. Mix handfuls of sugar into the soil around infected plants. This increases the numbers of bacteria that can fight the invasion.

You might be shocked to know that regular milk is an incredible fungus and virus fighter in the garden. Some plants such as tomatoes and roses are notorious for contracting nasty diseases that can kill the plant or limit fruit and flower production. Regularly add 1 tbsp. (15 mL) of powdered milk to the soil around your plants early in the season before you notice a problem. Alternatively, create a spray that can be applied to infected leaves using leftover or spoiled milk diluted with water.

Azaleas love acidic soil. Help your azaleas grow more beautiful than ever by occasionally watering plants with a mixture of 2 tbsp. (30 mL) white vinegar and 1-quart (1 L) water.

Use regular powdered cinnamon to combat bacterial or fungal infections such as powdery mildew on house plants. Lightly dust the powder onto the infected area. The area must be damp so that the cinnamon will stick. Be careful, too much can be damaging, so sprinkle lightly and do not pour it on in clumps.

To control slug outbreaks, fill up a plastic margarine or yogurt container with beer and partially bury it in the soil (with the top of the container level with the soil) near a plant that is being eaten by slugs. The slugs will be attracted to the beer where they will fall into the container and drown. Also plant rosemary between plants to keep slugs away.

Solutions 3

To keep rabbits out of the garden, combine (50/50) of talcum powder and ground hot pepper. Sprinkle around plants.

Stop Tomato Blossom End Rot: If your tomatoes are rotting from the bottom before you can harvest them they may not be getting enough calcium. Calcium deficiency is either caused by under-watering your tomato plants (allowing the soil to dry out for short periods of time) or by a calcium deficiency in the soil. To give your soil a calcium boost make a tea from crushed eggshells and pour it on the soil around the plant. To maintain moisture around tomato plants, water regularly and use a soda bottle drip irrigation system.

One of the best ways to provide a steady water supply to your plants without your constant attention is the gradual watering system or drip irrigation. The following contraption slowly feeds water into soil around the roots. Commercial watering spikes can also be purchased from you local garden center, however, using recycled materials, you can make your own drip irrigation system for free.

To make a simple watering device with a 2 L plastic bottle, drill 8 holes into the cap (not too small or holes will become clogged). Create a funnel by removing the bottom of the bottle, cutting vertically across with a sharp serrated knife, so that water can easily be replenished as well as catching rain water. Dig a hole next to a plant and bury one third of the bottle with the cap down; press dirt down around it. If the bottle is positioned among a group of plants it will be hidden from view. Pour water into the bottle until it is full. Fertilizer can be added to the bottle every few weeks if needed. Fill bottle once a day; make several bottles to place next to plants in the garden such as tomatoes that require lots of water.

- Blood and bone meal or a bulb-booster granular feed when planting does wonders for a newly planted bulb. **Warning**: Dogs and coyotes love the smell so do not use if you have dogs or coyotes around.

- If you have a problem with small rodents (voles, mice, shrews etc.) eating your bulbs from underneath, try laying small meshed chicken wire or hardware cloth under the bulbs, or use a wire "basket" so that only the growing tops of the bulbs are left open. Also, place chicken wire just under the soil line and secure it to prevent pests digging up bulbs.

Whiteflies, which attack many plants and spread disease, can be controlled: purée 2 garlic cloves, mix with 1 pint (570 mL) water, strain and spray on your plants. **Tip**: Attracting ladybugs is also effective for whitefly problems.

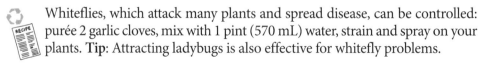

- Early morning is the ideal time to cut fresh flowers. The flowers have had the benefit of cool night air and the morning dew. Their stems are filled with water and carbohydrates and so are firm to the touch. As the day warms up, flowers gradually dehydrate. Midday is the worst time to cut, as transpiration rates are at a peak and plants are rapidly losing moisture through their leaves. Flowers become limp; their necks become bent. If cut, they will not recuperate well and their vase life will probably be short.

- When harvesting flowers, have a **plastic** bucket (metal can affect the pH balance of the water) of water on hand to put the flowers in. Work quickly; place cut flowers in the bucket immediately.

- Different types of flowers must be harvested at appropriate stages in their development. Flowers with multiple buds on each stem should have at least one bud showing color and one bud starting to open before being cut. This is true for spike flowers (salvias, agastaches, delphiniums, Eremurus, gladioli, snapdragons, stocks, larkspurs and the like) as well as cluster flowers (agapanthus, Alstroemeria, baby's breath, Clarkia, lilacs, phlox, Queen Anne's lace, verbenas, yarrow and silenes, for example). If gathered too early (while they're still tightly budded) these flowers will not open in a vase of water.

- By contrast, flowers that grow on individual stems (such as asters, calendulas, chrysanthemums, dahlias, Datura, gerbera daisies, marigolds, sunflowers, Tithonia and zinnias) should be cut when fully open.
  Tip: When selecting foliage, look for firm leaves and stems with strong colors.

 Reduce pests in the garden with this recipe: 1 tsp. (5 mL) vegetable oil, 1 tsp. (5 mL) biodegradable dish soap and 1-quart (1 L) water. Spray onto plants 3 times per week.

- Prolong the life of cut forget-me-nots, hyacinths and sweet peas by plunging the stems first into boiling water and then into cold water.

- Gladioli keep well in cold water. For curved tops, soak overnight.

- Place irises into cold water immediately after cutting.

Solutions 3

 To prolong the life of marguerites and marigolds, soak for 1-2 hours in 1 quart (1 L) of water with 1 tsp. (5 mL) peppermint oil.

 To keep peonies lasting longer, crush 3-4" (8-10 cm) of the stems and then set them in a mixture of 2 quarts (2 L) of water and 2 tsp. (10 mL) sugar.

- Place petunias in 2 quarts (2 L) water and add 2 tsp. (10 mL) salt.

- Fresh roses will last longer if you cut a 2" (5 cm) slit in the stems. If the roses aren't fresh, follow the same hint, but dip them in hot water before placing in a vase of cold water.

Strip the lower leaves from the stems of snapdragons, before putting them into a mixture of 2 quarts (2 L) water and 3 tbsp. (45 mL) baking soda.

- The best time to cut cattails is toward the end of August. Make sure there aren't many leaves on them. Place in a vase without water.

- Put the stems of tulips in boiling water for about 1 minute before sitting them in cool water.

- Remove the lower leaves from the stems of zinnias before placing them in 2 quarts (2 L) of water with 2 tbsp. (30 mL) of rock salt.

- If you want to preserve your flowers, place 1" (2.5 cm) of the stems in a mixture of equal parts of glycerin and water. Soak for 10 days.

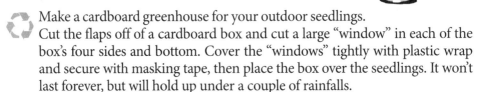

Make a cardboard greenhouse for your outdoor seedlings. Cut the flaps off of a cardboard box and cut a large "window" in each of the box's four sides and bottom. Cover the "windows" tightly with plastic wrap and secure with masking tape, then place the box over the seedlings. It won't last forever, but will hold up under a couple of rainfalls.

Fertilize your geraniums by adding dried coffee grounds to the soil around the plants.

If your green thumb extends to growing melons, try this to speed up the ripening process: Fill empty juice cans with water and place each melon on top of the can. During the day, the cans will collect solar heat and at night, when the melons ripen the best, the heat will help quicken the process. Leave as much of the lid on as possible so that the water won't leak out, just open the lid 1-2" (2.5-5 cm).

 Homemade Non-toxic Insecticide Recipe: Mix 2 cups (500 mL) flour and ½ cup (125 mL) buttermilk in 2 gallons (7.5 L) water. Spray this sticky solution on plant leaves to get rid of insects. Repeat every 10 days until the bugs are gone.

 Try picking bugs off of plants in the garden instead of using toxic pesticides. It may be more work, but it's just as effective.

 Make an alternative bug spray for soft-sided insects by mixing ½ cup (125 mL) biodegradeable dish soap in 16 cups (4 L) water. You can use soap flakes instead of liquid soap too. This is effective on aphids, mealy bugs and soft scale.

INSIDE PLANTS

 Choose houseplants such as the spider plant, which absorbs airborne toxins including smoke. Spider plants work well in office environments.

 For a natural fungicide and to help fight scale on houseplants, chop about 6 tomato leaves plus 1 onion and mix in ½ cup (125 mL) alcohol. Let sit for a few minutes and strain. Apply the solution with cotton balls.

 If you start bedding plants or herbs from seeds indoors, try placing an empty glass jar over the seedlings. This will act as a mini-greenhouse. To make sure the air circulates during the day, lift the jars slightly by using the jar lids as props.

 GREAT SELECTIONS FOR THE CUT FLOWER GARDEN

ANNUALS

Rocket Snapdragons, Bells of Ireland, Cosmos, Cockscomb, Celosia, Dahlia, Gladiolus, Globe Amaranth, Love-in-a-mist, Phlox, Dianthus, Statice, Strawflowers and Sunflower

PERENNIALS

Coneflowers, Rudebekia, Delphiniums, Lupins, Foxglove, Baby's Breath, Shasta Daisy, Dianthus, Carnations, Peonies, Asiatic Lilies, Iris, Hosta (for foliage), Yarrow and Asters

Solutions 3

Enjoy Cottage Time

There is nothing quite like cottage living. A vacationer noticed a sign that warned "DANGER! BEWARE OF DOG!" posted on the glass door of a little country store. Inside the store, a harmless-looking old hound dog was asleep on the floor by the cash register. "Is THAT the dog people are supposed to beware of?" he asked the store manager. "Yup." The man replied. The vacationer was amused. "That doesn't look like a dangerous dog to me. Why the sign?" "Well," the manager replied, "before I posted that sign, people kept tripping over him."

 Bring in the blooms and make them last! The Brooklyn Botanical Garden recommends a homemade mixture that they say works as well as the commercial variety of flower preservative. Mix 1 tsp. (5 mL) sugar, 1 tsp. (5 mL) 3% hydrogen peroxide and 2 tbsp. (30 mL) lemon or lime juice in 1-quart (1 L) warm water. Warm water is important because it's more easily absorbed. However, cold weather blooms, such as tulips, thrive in cold vase water.

 Zap poison ivy by combining: 1 gallon (4.5 L) apple cider vinegar, 1 cup (250 mL) table salt and 4 or 5 drops dish soap. Shake until salt is dissolved (so that the salt does not plug the nozzle) and put in a sprayer. Spray poison ivy, 2 or 3 times. **Beware**: This recipe will kill all greens. Treat poison ivy rash by rubbing the area with the rind and meat of watermelon. Air dry.

 Septic systems are designed for disposal of toilet wastes, tissue, soaps and water used from bathing, laundry and dishwashing. Disposing of improper solids in your septic can cause clogging and failure since the system can't break down the material. Dispose of solids such as cigarette butts, diapers, coffee grounds and grease in your household trash. **Extra Tip**: Use 1-ply toilet paper in your septic tank. **Another Extra Tip**: Do not pour any harmful chemicals, toxic substances, anti-bacterial soap, solvents, etc. into your septic system, purchase environmentally friendly products only.

- Instead of wooden spindles, enclose your deck with galvanized wire (2"/5 cm squares). Spray paint the wire with rust proof paint and staple it along the railing. Unique and nice to look at!

- Bonfires should be at least 60' (18 m) away from houses, trees, hedges, fences, sheds and motor vehicles. Avoid overhead power lines and make sure the bonfire is downwind of your spectator area.

- Open up your tum and say yum, yum, yum! S'more pancakes are easy to make. Take one pancake and put it on a plate sprinkle with chocolate chips and marshmallows, lay another pancake on top. Heat up over the bonfire, in the oven or microwave. Enjoy!

To soothe a bee sting, apply honey over affected area (now that's irony). *Submitted by Henry Magnusson*

If you get bit by a black fly, soak yourself in a baking soda bath. Use about 1 cup (250 mL) for a full tub to help ease the itchiness. Next, cut a garlic clove in half and rub on the bite. "You won't smell great, but it helps ease the itch and 'cuts the poison,' as my grandmother insisted." *Submitted by Pat Cole*

Ouch! Little Tina has her first mosquito bite of the season. Rub a small amount of Thousand Island salad dressing onto the area to stop the itch.

Introducing Lavender Oil: Insect bites can be terribly irritating, especially for young skin. Lavender essential oil can be applied directly to any itchy or sore bites to help ease the discomfort. Lavender is one of the few essential oils that is safe to use undiluted directly on the skin. Lavender oil comes from the flowers of common lavender bushes known as lavendula angustifolia, lavendula officinalis or lavendula vera. It is a powerful antiseptic and is used externally as an excellent restorative and tonic. When rubbed on temples, for example, it can cure a nervous headache and it is also a soothing addition to bathwater. It's powerful antiseptic properties are able to kill many common bacteria and is as well a powerful antidote to some snake venoms. Lavender oil is very useful in the treatment of burns, sunburns and scalds and is frequently an ingredient in incense, potpourri and insect repellent. Lavender can also help prevent the formation of permanent scar tissue.

Lavender

Green Tip: Turn off the water heater in your cottage when you leave. It wastes energy to keep water hot when it isn't needed. It doesn't take long to heat up when you return.

Solutions 3

Green Hints for Feeding Creatures both Inside and Out

Attracting wildlife is a rewarding experience. Before taking the steps to bring new friends to your yard, keep in mind that wildlife is truly wild and unpredictable. Ask yourself; do you really want more wildlife around than you already have? If the answer is "yes," get ready for these smart ideas!

If you want to encourage rabbits, squirrels, chipmunks and other small critters to frequent your yard, you must provide food, shelter and water. A water garden or pond will attract many types of wildlife. A short tray of water or ground-level birdbath is a great place to start.

Chipmunks: There are 21 chipmunk species in North America. To lure chipmunks to your garden consider planting a variety of fruit, nut or seed producing trees and shrubs. Examples are: Beaked hazel, sweet fern, dogwoods, maples, bitternut hickory, white elm, buffalo berry, blueberries, cherries, raspberries, viburnums and American basswood. Provide chipmunks with nesting sites by adding rock or brush piles or old logs. Unlike squirrels, chipmunks pose few problems at bird feeders.

Butterflies: A ceramic or glass pie plate, plastic or terra cotta plant saucer, or a dish with a sloping rim can be used to make butterfly feeders. Suspend the plate with flowerpot hangers or fashion a macramé style holder from household twine. Wind the holder with silk or plastic flowers to decorate the butterfly feeder and make it visually appealing to butterflies. Hang the feeder from the bough of a shady tree, in a spot where you can easily view butterflies. Place the feeder a little higher than your highest flowers. Add slices of over-ripe fruit. You can sprinkle a little fruit juice or water over the fruit slices if they dry out (it's the mushy, rotting, very over-ripe fruit that butterflies like best). Replace the fruit if it dries out or becomes moldy.

Birds: If you do not want to purchase bird feed and hang a feeder, you can attract birds of various types by planting different plants. Sunflowers will attract many birds, as will coneflower and thistle plants.

Hummingbirds: Using red dye in the hummingbird feeder is not necessary. Red food dye has been suspected of promoting tumor development in hummingbirds. The jury is still out on the subject, but until red food dye has been proven safe for hummingbirds, it is a good idea to stay clear of it. If your feeder is not red, you can place red stickers on it to catch their attention.

Hummingbird Food Recipe: Combine 1 part sugar and 4 parts boiled water. Cool and add to feeder. Replace food every 3-5 days.

Orioles: Attract orioles with nectar, nuts, suet and fruits such as oranges, cherries, apples, pears, bananas and even grape jelly. Platform or tray feeders often work best. Be sure to hang feeders from a tree branch or place on deck rail instead of on the ground.

Bird Pancake Recipe: Beat 2 small eggs, stir in 1 cup (250 mL) milk, 1 cup (250 mL) grated zucchini, 1 cup (250 mL) grated carrot and 3½ tbsp. (47 mL) cooking oil. In a separate bowl, combine 1 cup (250 mL) whole-wheat flour, 3 tsp. (15 mL) baking powder, 2 tbsp. (30 mL) sugar and 1½ cups (375 mL) cornmeal. Stir together all ingredients until slightly lumpy. Pour into a frying pan and brown both sides. Cool and serve. Freeze leftovers.

Bluebirds: What a treat to see bluebirds in the yard! They prefer to nest in boxes on a tree stump or wooden fence post between 3 and 5' (.90 and 1.5 m) high. Bluebirds also nest in abandoned woodpecker nest holes. The most important measurement is the hole diameter, 1½" (3.8 cm) is small enough to deter starlings. Starlings and house sparrows have been known to kill baby bluebirds as well as adults sitting on the nest. Bluebirds tend to have problems with other animals too. The easiest way to discourage predatory cats, snakes, raccoons and chipmunks is to mount the house on a metal pole or use a metal predator guard on a wood post.

Dragonflies: Creating a new pond in your garden is a great way to attract dragonflies with fast results. Make sure that less than 30% of your pond is shade covered. Dragonfly larvae are cold blooded so they need sunlight. Without enough heat they are inactive and stop breeding, eating or escaping from predators. Adult dragonflies are solar-powered and need to reach a certain temperature before they can fly. **Tip**: If you are attracting dragonflies to control mosquitoes, be sure that you do not use bug zappers as they will zap also your dragonflies.

Deer: People interested in feeding deer in their yard, should select a high protein food supplement. Corn only has 6% protein versus what deer actually need: a 16-20% protein food. Corn only offers the deer a low protein, high carbohydrate diet (basically deer candy). Feeding the low protein corn makes the deer prone to munching shrubs in the yard. **Note**: Although beautiful to look at, deer can do a lot of damage to flower and vegetable gardens. Be sure you can deal with that before enticing them into the yard. Of course, if deer do not live in your area due to lack of habitat like woods, you will not get any in your yard. People who live near major roadways should not entice them as the danger of accidents and deaths will increase.

Rabbit Food: Purée and mix 1 small carrot, half banana and 1 tbsp. (15 mL) honey. Add ¼ cup (60 mL) of both ground-up (use a coffee grinder) rabbit pellets and ¼ cup (60 mL) ground-up oats. Mix and knead. Cover with parchment paper. Press out "dough" in ¼" (.25 cm) thick layer. Use a tumbler to cut into circles. Place cut shapes onto a parchment paper covered cookie sheet. Bake at 325°F (160° C) for about 20 minutes (check to make sure they are not browning). Turn off the heat and let the cookies sit in the warm oven for an hour.

 Hamster Food: Combine the following in a small dish: 3 pieces cut up carrot, 1 cut up carrot top, ½ cup (125 mL) Cheerios, ½ cup (125 mL) unsalted sunflower seeds, ½ cup (125 mL) raisins, 4 small apple slices, 1 cut up cabbage leaf.

 Dog Treats: In a large bowl, stir together 2 cups (500 mL) whole-wheat flour, 1 cup (250 mL) cornmeal and 1 tbsp. (15 mL) salt. Mix in ⅓ cup (75 mL) vegetable oil, one egg and ¾-1 cup (175-250 mL) water. Knead to form soft dough (add flour if needed). Cut into 2" (5 cm) circles. Bake on a greased cookie sheet at 350°F (180°C) for 20 minutes. Cool and store in airtight container.

 Dog Food: In a pot combine 3 lbs. (1.4 kg) minced chicken meat, 2½ cups (625 mL) frozen minced vegetable blend, 4 cups (1 L) rice and 6½ cups (1.54 L) water. Bring to a boil, stir constantly. Reduce heat and simmer until rice is tender and all liquid has been absorbed. Cool and store in fridge. **Tip**: Avoid giving dogs chocolate, broccoli, brussel sprouts, beans, turnip, cabbage, onions, peppers, tomato, spinach, garlic and cucumber.

 Cat Snack: Combine 2 eggs, 1 tbsp. (15 mL) milk, 3 tbsp. (45 mL) cottage cheese and 2 tbsp. (30 mL) alfalfa sprouts, finely chopped. Pour into a hot pan with 1 tbsp. (15 mL) vegetable oil or butter. When brown at bottom, turn over and brown other side. Cut and serve.

 Here is a warning from a concerned Saskatchewan resident:
I save rainwater in 45 gallon (170 L) plastic barrels and I like to have open tops so I can scoop the water out with a bucket for flushing the toilet and watering etc. (I also salvage my laundry water and reuse it for flushing the toilet). I learned a hard lesson when I returned from a week away and found a deceased red squirrel in a barrel that was half-full of water. It had fallen in and couldn't climb out and drowned. I had forgotten to put a 2x4" into the barrel so any squirrel that happened to fall into the water could not climb out. Normally, I also tie the wood down so it does not float up and out. Cheers, Dick

Heartfelt Green Ways to Love Your Pet

"We can judge the heart of a man by his treatment of animals." *Immanual Kant*

- Pet hair on furniture can be removed by using one of the following techniques: Wipe with a rubber glove, the side of a tennis shoe, a rubber jar opener, sticky lint brush, a wet rag or a stiff brush. Or wrap duct tape around your fingers and push your hand along furniture to pickup hair or vacuum.

- To get your pet to eat medicine, break off a small piece of bread and hide the medicine inside. Feed the bread to him/her and watch him eat it so that you are sure the medicine wasn't dropped.

- To prevent a pet bowl from sliding on the floor, cut a square of rubberized shelf fabric larger than the bowl and place it underneath the pet dish. *Submitted by Diane Leitold*

- Avoid using metal water dishes for outside pets; the risk is that their tongue can stick to the frozen metal. In the summer, metal bowls get very hot and may burn your dog.

- Store big bags of dry dog food in a clean garbage can with a lid. Plastic ice-cream pails are a convenient size for smaller amounts of food.

- Save the water from cooked vegetables to mix with your dog's dry food. It adds extra flavor and vitamins.

- **Dog Shampoo**: Combine: 2 oz. (56.7 g) dish soap, 16 oz. (454 g) water, 16 oz. (454 g) apple cider vinegar and 2 oz. (56 g) glycerin. Mix together, wash and rinse.

- **Dog Breath Freshener Recipe 1**: Combine 1 cup (250 mL) wheat flour, ¼ tsp. (1 mL) salt and 1½ tbsp. (7 mL) charcoal (found in most health food stores). In another bowl, combine 1 egg, 2 tbsp. (30 mL) cooking oil, ¼ cup (60 mL) chopped parsley and 4 tsp. (20 mL) fresh mint. Stir in the flour mixture plus ⅓ cup (75 mL) milk until the dough has the consistency of bread dough (add more flour as needed). Drop by spoonfuls onto baking sheet. Bake for 15 minutes at 350°F (180°C).

- **Dog Breath Freshener Recipe 2**: In a bowl, combine ¼ cup (60 mL) fresh mint, 1 egg, 2 tsp. (10 mL) flax seed oil, ¾ cup (175 mL) milk and ⅛ cup (30 mL) wheat germ. Mix. Continue mixing and gradually add 3 cups (750 mL) flour (until the dough is not sticky). Roll out and cut doggie cookies ¼" (1 cm) thick. Bake 30 minutes at 350°F (180°C).

If dog breath is a problem for your pet, mix parsley in with his/her food once a day. Often plaque is the culprit causing your pet's yucky breath. On that note, pets should have their teeth brushed too! If the breath problem persists see your vet, it may be time for Rusty to visit the dentist.

To prevent fleas from bothering your dog, place chamomile leaves in the dog-house or put garlic in your dog's food.

- Put 1 tsp. (5 mL) of cider vinegar in your female dog's water every time you change it. Doing this will neutralize the acid in his/her urine and in then it will not burn your lawn as badly.

- To get your puppy's attention, put a few pennies in an empty pop can and shake. The noise will make him stop what he is doing. This can be a good training tool. **Tip**: Discourage pets from chewing on electrical chords by wiping them with a bar of soap (the chord not the pet).

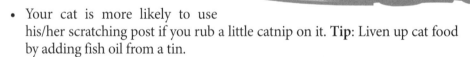

- Your cat is more likely to use his/her scratching post if you rub a little catnip on it. **Tip**: Liven up cat food by adding fish oil from a tin.

Make a disposable kitty litter pan using the empty box that comes with 24 cans of pop.

- To keep cat litter fresh smelling, mix baby powder in with the litter. *Submitted by Eric Kidd*

- Hamsters live alone and should not be rooming together in one cage or they will fight. The exception to this rule, is if you are breeding a male and female, otherwise two or more in the same cage, or near each other, could have a very sad result.

- Chewing is an integral part of a parrot's everyday life. In the wild, nuts and wood make up a large part of their chewing habits. A bird's beak grows constantly throughout his/her life; chewing helps keep beaks trim and healthy. Birds are also very intelligent and need this constant stimulation and entertainment to be happy. Bird toys are meant to be destroyed! Don't be upset if your bird goes through lots of toys, on the contrary this means your bird is happy. **Tip**: Purchase a second bird or mounting a mirror in the cage will keep budgies quieter.

- If you suffer from allergies, consider a pet snake as they have no dander, hair or fleas. Another big advantage that snakes have over cats and dogs is that you don't have to feed them daily. Supply them with fresh water to drink and feed them according to their species type. Lastly, you don't have to clean up after them everyday.

- Before you buy a fish, bring a cup full of your tap water to your local pet store and ask to have the water tested for pH and hardness. If you are short on time, you will probably prefer to buy fish that thrive in your water type, rather than spending your evenings trying to adjust the water to the fish.

 To get rid of fleas, try making this flea powder using the following natural ingredients: 2 oz. (56 g) dried pennyroyal (a dried herb extract), 1 oz. (28 g) wormwood, 1 oz. (28 g) rosemary and a healthy dash of cayenne pepper. Mix together and store in a labeled container. Use on your pet as needed.

To make a **flea collar**, soak a thin strip of terry towel in a mixture of boiling water and about ⅓ cup (75 mL) rosemary. Let the towel dry and then sew a Velcro fastener on the collar. Save the leftover mixture to use as rinse after you've bathed your pet.

Dear Reena,

We add a new cat (usually seniors) to our household when one passes away. Of course, they come with their habits. There was one that was always scratching the rug, even though I have at least three scratching posts of different heights in the house. Once I actually opened my eyes, it all made sense! The scratching post is usually made with carpet. This carpet was exactly the same texture as my floor carpet. I then purchased two different sisal scratching posts instead, (my girlfriend found a "log" one with rope wound around the wood). Now when the cats go to the rug, I pick them up and take them to the post and make scratching motions on the new post. I also rub catnip all over. It only takes a few days before they catch on.

Submitted by Chris Pratt

Solutions 3

Bird Brained Green Schemes to Keep your Feathered Friends Happy

One of the chief benefits of a luscious and beautiful yard is the fact that it can provide a home to all sorts of creatures, including some of the most beautiful birds in the neighborhood.

- If birds are constantly making unwanted nests underneath your roof line, hang a curtain of aluminum foil, plastic sheeting or sheet metal from a wire strung just above where the roof overhang meets the wall.

- To remove bird droppings from a car, apply cold water until it is soft enough to remove with a washing mitt without scratching the paintwork. Do not use hot water as temperature can act as a catalyst to the chemical reactions between droppings and lacquer. Next gently apply baby shampoo and water to clean the spot. Some people apply extra wax to the car roof so that bird droppings wipe off with great ease.

- If birds constantly fly into your windows, apply a cover to the inside of the window or close the curtains so that the bird no longer sees its own reflection and loses interest in the area.

- Landscaping for birds begins with trees and bushes and the right flowers. It's not the blossoms themselves that most birds want. Birds want the seeds that come later.

Plant some of the following flowers to attract birds to your garden this summer: aster, calendula, cockscomb, coreopsis, cornflower, cosmos, larkspur, portulaca, purple coneflower, snapdragon, sunflower and one of my favorite flowers, zinnia.

Consider purchasing a birdbath for the garden, keeping in mind that birds feel more secure using a birdbath that is surrounded by plants, shrubbery and trees. Birdbaths should be kept free from algae, bird droppings and other debris. They can be sterilized using a mixture of 4½ cups (1.2 L) water and ½ cup (125 mL) 3% hydrogen peroxide or white vinegar. Be sure to rinse thoroughly.

- To keep squirrels off of a pole mounted bird feeder, put a stovepipe or 4-6" (10-15 cm) diameter PVC pipe around the pole (from the bottom). They can't wrap their paws around the pipe and won't be able to climb up the pole. You can also put a piece of PVC pipe around the chain if your feeder is a hanging type.

- Make a bird feeder by filling am empty mesh onion bag with suet (leftover fat). **Tip**: Birds also love Cheerios!

- Save dryer lint and put it near trees for birds to collect and make nests.

- Some of the best summer blossoms for keeping those spring hummingbirds coming back include bleeding hearts, petunias, trumpet honeysuckle, trumpet vines, impatiens and morning glories.

- Birds aren't just here for their good looks. Birds such as barn swallows and purple martins are capable of eating pounds of mosquitoes and other insects. They are not the only species of birds that are known for their insect eating; robins, mockingbirds, chickadees, nuthatches and woodpeckers are just a few of the many species that are voracious insect eaters. Birds can be attracted with birdhouses or nest boxes. Don't worry that birds will fill up on food and not eat insects; most birds need insects to feed their young who are incapable of digesting seeds. No matter how well stocked your feeder; insects provide birds with critical amounts of fat, protein and potassium that they need to survive.

- Make your own bird feeder: Slice an orange or grapefruit in half, punch three holes equally spaced around the rim about ¼" (1 cm) down. Hang from a tree branch with string or twine and fill with birdseed. To make the feeder even more user friendly, poke a stick through the middle to serve as a perch.

- To get a bird to bathe, use a plastic paint tray. The tray allows your bird to venture into the water gradually and at his own pace. Also, there are little raised areas on the bottom of the tray, which provide traction.

- If you have a bird that has flown into flypaper, the best way to get the bird off and to get the gooey gunk off is to apply peanut butter to it.

- Pigeon problems? Screen the birds out from wall recesses and window ledges with fine-mesh chicken wire sold at hardware and garden shops. Also, sheets of plastic with plastic spikes at narrow intervals are available in hardware shops for use on flat roofs or window ledges. It is impossible for pigeons to perch on them or find a comfortable foothold.

Solutions 3

Ways to Reduce the Mosquito Population

No one likes being bit by mosquitoes? We also can't tolerate the annoying shrill buzzing sound? Getting stressed-out while trying to smack a mosquito during the night? Well, the bad news is that in many areas mosquitoes are here to stay but the good news it that we can reduce the amount of bites with the following helpful hints.

- Step 1 is easy! Empty all containers that hold water. You would not believe the small amount of water it takes for mosquitoes to grow and develop. Things like buckets, tires, flower pots, wheel barrows, pop cans, beer bottles, coffee cans, bird feeders, bird baths and anything else that can hold water needs to be cleaned and emptied regularly. Additionally, make sure all gutters drain well. **Extra Tip**: Keep grass cut short and the banks of running streams free from weeds.

- Step 2 is also easy! If you want to avoid insecticides, protective clothing is your best option: Wear loose-fitting, tightly woven material with long sleeves and pants. **Joel's Tip** (see page 68): Head gear or full body suits made of mosquito netting work well.

- Ornamental ponds tend to become mosquito breeding grounds. You can keep the mosquito larvae population under control by stocking your pond with bright, exotic fish or with less exotic small native fish which are not as susceptible to bird predation. Another option is to add a pump to agitate the water. Mosquitoes will not breed in moving water.

- Change the water in your bird bath once a week and you'll never, ever have to worry about mosquitoes forming in the bath. Check rain barrels for mosquito larvae. A tight cover or screening will prevent egg laying. A thin layer of vegetable oil will kill mosquitoes already present.

- To prevent mosquitoes from breeding in bird baths, toss in Bacillus thuringiensis 'Israelensis' (Bti), available at garden retailers as mosquito dunks. Neither will hurt plants, pets or even beneficial insects. Bti is a naturally occurring soil bacterium that can effectively kill mosquito larvae present in water. Bti is also used for controlling forestry pests.

- Fill ornamental pools with minnows or goldfish (they eat mosquito larvae on the water surface) or treat the pools with biological larvicide's (chemicals or natural bacteria that can be used to kill mosquito larvae).

- Be informed! Most provinces and states have a health website showing the number of human cases of West Nile virus for each year.

- Citronella oil is the trendiest repellent these days. In stores, you'll find citronella candles, citronella incense and citronella wrist bands. It is not very effective. If a group is huddled around a picnic table, a candle or two may help somewhat, but if there is a breeze citronella looses its effect.

There are several types of plants that naturally repel mosquitoes. Some of these are horsemint, marigold, catnip and rosemary. **Extra Tip**: You can also use lemon eucalyptus oil as mosquito repellent.

One of the most renowned natural enemies of mosquitoes is garlic; they can't stand the scent of it. Pinch a garlic clove, to get its liquid running and then rub it over exposed skin. Or eat garlic in large quantities so that the scent literally comes through your pores. There are mosquito repellents to spray on lawns whose main ingredient is a garlic liquid concentrate. Garlic can also be grown in the garden to repel female mosquito (these are the ones that bite, because they need the blood to produce eggs) and to seek easier prey elsewhere.

- It is said that one small brown bat can catch 600 mosquitoes per hour. You might want to consider building or buying a bat house. If you are worried about contracting rabies from the bats you attract, consider the Niagara Frontier Wildlife Habitat Council's statistic that less than half of 1% of all bats contract rabies, which all mammals can do, "they normally bite only in self-defense and pose little threat to people who do not handle them."

- The purple martin is a beautiful bird to watch and listen to. These birds can eat up to 6,000 mosquitoes and insects a day.

- Keep it breezy. Mosquitoes don't like strong wind currents. When company drops by and you want to sit outside, position a fan next to the seating area to keep the little pests away.

- The DEET Debate: Insect repellents containing DEET (N,N-diethyl meta-toluamide) are the most common repellents used but before applying it remember that skin is porous: Whatever is smeared onto skin will be absorbed into your body. DEET provides short-term protection when applied to skin and clothing and is effective against most biting flies, mosquitoes, fleas and ticks. Canadian products can have a concentration of up to 30% DEET. Health Canada recommends applying concentrations of up to 30% for adults and 6% to 10% for children. If choosing to use DEET read and follow the label directions. Avoid applying DEET on children's hands and fingers as they may ingest it. Drinking DEET can be fatal.

- Mosquitoes are attracted to us (or any other blood meal source) by our breath; heat and carbon dioxide. Devices claiming to lure mosquitoes to their death by CO_2 indeed do just that, they lure the mosquitoes by converting propane gas into CO_2 and then capture them in various ways, depending on the product. If using such a trap or device, place them in shaded areas far away from human activity since they can draw in large numbers of mosquitoes. Depending on the model and size, most devices claim to cover an area somewhere between ¾-1½ acres (32,000-65,000 sq. ft). An Internet search for mosquito magnets, traps or devices will give you an assortment of products to browse through. Before purchasing a device, remember that many flying creatures (not just mosquitoes) may be attracted to the machine.

- Although it is not a 100% natural insect repellent, Avon's Skin So Soft does contain mineral and carrot seed oils. Many women stand by the product's results. **Extra Tip**: Orange or lemon peels, Vicks Vapor Rub or Listerine will also help keep mosquitoes away. Rub on exposed skin when outside.

- Some say that catnip oil is 10 times more effective than DEET and completely safe on humans. You be the judge, buy catnip oil and make a spray or purchase repellents with catnip oil as an ingredient.

- Most importantly, stay inside if possible during the hours of dusk and dawn when mosquitoes are most active.

A huge thank-you to Joel Gosselin who had a pest control company in Winnipeg, MB for 29 years and sent in great feedback on what does and doesn't work.

Practical Ways to Deal with Cankerworms, Cutworms and Moths

We want to make "green" choices but some creatures bring a whole new meaning to the word challenge. The time has come to bite back!

- Tree tangle foot is a sticky material used to repel insect pests. Spread on the bark of trees to control gypsy moths, cankerworms, climbing cutworms and ants. Tangle foot is made from natural gum resins, castor oil and vegetable waxes. Do not put it all the way around plant trunks, it will girdle and can kill plants.

- If you can determine that there are no egg masses in a tree, or if you have sprayed the tree, you may be able to prevent migrating caterpillars from climbing up the trunk by the use of barriers. Construct a barrier band around the trunk made of duct tape, tin foil or tarpaper and coat it generously with grease petroleum jelly. Never apply grease directly to the tree bark. The barrier band should be in the shade or you run the risk of killing the bark and cambium under the band. Check the barrier band daily to see if more grease is necessary. Remove the band in early July after the caterpillars have formed cocoons.

- If you locate the foliage that cankerworms are feeding on, you can spray with these insecticides: Dipel, Thuricide, Bactur, Biological Worm Killer or use the super-safe, organically approved Bacillus thuringiensis insecticide. Bacillus requires a several day waiting period before the worm actually dies, even though they cease feeding activities immediately. **Note**: Freezing weather just prior to, during and following hatching will kill many of the young caterpillars.

- Cocoons may be difficult to remove using water pressure. Brush them off the house with a stiff broom. Bag, burn, bury or compost the cocoons.

- To protect an area such as a garden, build a 24" (61 cm) tall enclosure of plastic sheeting and secure its lower edge so that caterpillars cannot crawl underneath. Spray the sheeting with vegetable oil to prevent the caterpillars from climbing the wall. Repeat oil application daily, or as often as needed.

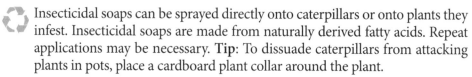

 Insecticidal soaps can be sprayed directly onto caterpillars or onto plants they infest. Insecticidal soaps are made from naturally derived fatty acids. Repeat applications may be necessary. **Tip:** To dissuade caterpillars from attacking plants in pots, place a cardboard plant collar around the plant.

DID YOU KNOW? Spraying will only reduce this year's population of caterpillars so why bother? Moths from untreated areas will likely fly in and lay eggs on treated trees later this year. Next years population of caterpillars won't be affected, by this years control technique.

- There is no question that it is no longer recommended to keep mothballs in the home due to health and poison concerns. However, it is interesting to note that mothballs do not repel, they kill moths, eggs and larvae if the air around the garment is saturated and the space is airtight. If you choose to store fabric and mothballs together, be prepared for clothing to carry a mothball odor after they are taken out of storage.

- Certain moths love to attack. Fabric stored woolens should be wrapped in clean paper, as the fabrics are packed into tightly sealed trunks or boxes. It is important to maintain the highest possible concentration of Moth Guard or cedar chips inside the plastic bag containing the susceptible items. Cedar closets and most cedar chests are ineffective because a sufficiently tight seal is rarely maintained.

- Mothproofing is often accomplished by a special treatment during the manufacture of woolen fabric or other susceptible items. Using a dry cleaning service is a good way of treating fabrics. One of the most effective ways to get rid of moths, (especially clothes moths) is to regulate the humidity of your home. **Tip:** Ironing your clothes will help get rid of clothes moths infestation.

Moths are repelled by strong smelling herbs. Lavender, wormwood, cedar or patchouli along with a small amount of rosemary, cinnamon, cloves or tansy work well. Mix any combination and place in the toe of a used stocking. Tie open end and hang in closet or place in a drawer.

- Place leftover soap slivers into a vented plastic bag rather than using dangerous smelly mothballs. Place the seasonal clothes into the bag and pack them away. Fabrics will smell and great and stay protected.

 Blanket Mothproofing Recipe: Combine 6 tbsp. (90 mL) eucalyptus oil, 2 cups (500 mL) denatured alcohol, 2 cups (500 mL) soap flakes into a jar and shake. Add 1 tsp. (5 mL) solution to 1 gallon (4.5 L) warm water. Soak blanket (do not rinse). Hang blanket to dry.

- Pantry moths can be found in rice, pasta, cake mixes, rat or mouse bait, breakfast cereals, children's artwork (containing pasta, corn, etc.), herbs, spices, grain, feed, seed, dried vegetables (decorative or edible) or dried fruit! Vacuum all shelves/floors and wash with vinegar and water. Throw out all grains that you suspect has been infected by larvae. If you bring any grain based products into the house, immediately put them in the freezer for four days before putting them away in the pantry. This will kill any eggs or larvae that are already inside. Store food in airtight containers, which are made of hard plastic, glass or metal (not plastic bags). **Tip**: The best way to determine whether a container is airtight is to fill it up with water, flip it upside down and see if it leaks.

- If you have frequent moth problems, consider permanently storing all of your grain based products in the freezer instead of the pantry. Sprinkle lavender chips or cedar chips in cupboards to prevent moths from invading. **Note**: Most of the moth control products on the market are moth poisons, moth traps and mothballs. Mothballs are not a healthy product to keep in the home, especially near food.

Cutworm Protectors: If your transplants are being chewed in half near the roots by an unknown assailant, you likely have cutworms; the larvae stage of a moth that inhabit the soil surface feeding on fresh, succulent stems. One method of controlling this hungry worm is a simple barrier device made of scrap materials. Cut a toilet paper roll tube in half and place it around the stem of your seedling when you plant. Press the tube into the soil halfway. The paper tube will act as a barrier between your plant's delicate stem and the jaws of the cutworm.

- Another alternative is to cut the ends off the plastic containers that transplants come in and place them around the stems of each seedling. **Note**: Plastic will not degrade, so you will need to cut the collars off once the plants are established and all risk of cutworm damage is past.

Conquer Ants

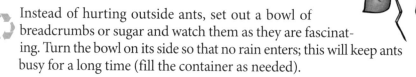

Ants are one of the most important contributors to a yard's health we need ants in our yards and gardens! They rid it of detritus, protect the plants from some pests and improve soil conditions. However, depending on the type of ants that you have, they can bite, get into your food, cause allergic reactions and build mounds in the garden. There are several ways to combat ants, some are "green" and some are not. Both are listed – the choice is yours.

Instead of hurting outside ants, set out a bowl of breadcrumbs or sugar and watch them as they are fascinating. Turn the bowl on its side so that no rain enters; this will keep ants busy for a long time (fill the container as needed).

- If you don't find ants as cute and cuddly as a three-year-old boy does here are a few alternatives: Place rhubarb leaves on ant hills or prepare:
  Rhubarb Tea: boil rhubarb leaves in water and pour over ant hills. Rhubarb leaves are poisonous and once positioned on a hill they will be carried to the queen. **Tip**: If ants are entering your home, lay cucumber peelings under door frames at doorways and basement window frames

Create liquid bait by mixing 1 tsp. (5 mL) boric acid with 2½ oz. (70 g) corn syrup. Heat until the boric acid dissolves. Saturate cotton balls with the solution and put into jars. In theory the ants will take the food back to the queen.

- Cover the colony with hot pepper flakes (not liquid sauce) and several types of powdery pepper flavoring and within a few hours the entire colony should disappear. Ants are irritated by hot pepper. **Tip**: Paprika also works.

- Leave cola inside of a 2 L pop bottle. Ants get in, but they can't get out.

- Another natural deterrent to an invasion of ants is the planting of mint (bearing in mind that mint is a very invasive plant and may take over more of your garden than you would like). If the mint plant proves too aggressive for you, brew a strong mint tea to create a natural insecticide and pour it on the mound.

- Diatomaceous earth, available at swimming pool supply stores, is one chemical proven to kill ants. Sprinkle diatomaceous earth around mounds and across the path of the ants to dehydrate them.

Ant Deterrent: mix ½ cup (125 mL) water with 15 drops peppermint oil and 10 drops citronella oil. Cut cotton strips and soak them in the solution. Hang them up outside on trees, shrubs or in windows.

- Purchase pipe tobacco from your local store. Soak it in warm water overnight. While wearing gloves throw away the soggy tobacco. Pour the liquid over the anthill.

- Certain types of ants, won't return if you wipe an ant trail with vinegar.

- Fill a spray bottle with 50/50 water and rubbing alcohol, spray anthills. A stronger concentration is even more effective.

- Keep ants out by doing your part. Seal your home, caulk openings and fill holes.

- Artificial sweeteners will zap ants as well as yellow cornmeal. Open three packages and sprinkle the mounds.

- Keep ants out! Buy the cheapest bag of corn flakes and make a tiny hole in the bag. Let the air out by placing it on the floor and walking all over it until you just have a bag of small sawdust size corn flakes. Spread this where ever you have an ant problem, around trees, the lawn, house and yard. An added benefit is that when ants find an abundance of food outside they will not enter into your house.

- For very hardy ants that are taking over your home, drastic measures are required. You will need ant poison and it needs to be applied often as these ants are very resilient. Make sure that you are not purchasing ant repellent but instead ant poison. The correct poison (make sure that no kids or pets can get into it) will have a picture of an ant on the front and lasts 6 weeks. Or combine dish soap and boiling water and pour it into the ant holes each day for at least 3 days. If you are desperate purchase Raid Ant Killer – it has a 2-week residual kill.

- A border of cayenne pepper, paprika, chili powder, cream of tartar or dried peppermint will keep ants out of your flowerbeds or garden.

Warning: Use caution around children and pets, some of the points listed above are poisonous!

Cute Stinky Skunks

Say this 5 times fast: A skunk sat on a stump. The stump thought the skunk stunk. The skunk thought the stump stunk. What stunk the skunk or the stump?

If you see a skunk stamping his front feet, take heed; he is warning you and you better run. Dogs ignore this warning which is why they are more likely to get sprayed.

- Skunks are nocturnal; therefore they are most likely to be seen at night and early morning when they're out scavenging for food. Skunks can and do eat anything; bird eggs, bugs and larvae, human waste, small rodents and garbage.

- Never surprise a skunk! If you do not like to be startled then imagine how skunks feel when they are surprised by humans. If you know skunks are around your area, be cautious. Turn on outside lights. Make noise while walking to your car so that they know that you are on the way.

- Skunks have very poor eyesight but loud music and motion lights make skunks feel as though they are being watched and chances are they will pack their bags and leave if they sense danger.

- In general, skunks left alone will wander away, but when skunks make their home underneath or around yours, they may need to be removed with a box-design live trap or you may need to call in a professional. A live trap should be a solid shape with a single entrance (about 7-10"/18-25 cm square and 30"/76 cm long). When set, the entrance door is locked up in place to allow a skunk to enter the trap. When the skunk steps on a false floor in the trap, the door closes behind the skunk. Live traps for skunks may be purchased from hardware stores or you can construct a trap using wood. Some commercial live traps are made of open mesh and should be enclosed with tin or light plywood before use to allow easy handling with little risk of the skunk spraying. **Tip**: Skunks do not generally spray in enclosed spaces. A trap containing a skunk should be gently picked up and driven to another location at least 7 miles (12 km) away.

  - Skunks are easy to catch in live traps. Use sardines, tuna or moist cat food as bait. Place the bait inside, at the back of the trap. When the skunk tries to get the bait, the trap door closes and captures them. Make sure you have caught a skunk and not a cat or other small animal before moving the animal. Live traps should have an inspection hole in the top for identifying the animal.

    Tomato Juice Theory: Bathe your dog in tomato juice to remove skunk smell? Some say it works while others disagree. In any case, choosing an alternative method

will lessen the mess, expense of tomato juice and possibility of stains on clothing and floors.

 For pets that have been sprayed by a skunk, bathe the animal in a mixture of 1-quart (1 L) 3% hydrogen peroxide, ¼ cup (60 mL) baking soda (sodium bicarbonate) and 1 tsp. (5 mL) liquid detergent. After five minutes, rinse the animal with water. Repeat if necessary. The mixture must be used up after mixing and will not work if it is stored for any length of time. (Taken from *Household Solutions 2 with Kitchen Secrets*). **Tip**: Vinegar and water (½ and ½) are not as effective but may also be used; be sure to avoid the face.

- You don't need to burn or throw away clothes or other items that have been skunked. Soak in vinegar then biodegradable dish soap. Use laundry detergent and dry in the sun until the last trace of odor is gone. Fresh air and sun are the key elements!

An organic cleaning product called Orange TKO will remove skunk odor from the barn and from clothing. Orange TKO is made from orange peels and is a concentrate that is diluted in water. Soak washable fabrics in 2 oz. (56 g) TKO per 1 gallon (4 L) of water for a few hours or overnight and then wash as usual.

Attempting to drive your skunky smelling car? After cleaning the car out with vinegar and water or TKO, place an open bag of charcoal inside the vehicle to absorb excess smell.

- Skunks in the garden are not necessarily a bad thing. They will eat every insect that you don't want eating your garden. If skunks are raiding your garden or flowerbed it is likely they are not after your plants, but the insects in the soil. The trouble is that while they hunt for bugs they may make a mess of the whole area. Remember, if they are startled, they can make a big stink! There are a variety of skunk repellents available at home and garden stores.

- If you have garbage around, clean it up. Put dog and cat food in covered airtight containers. Leaving out pet food is an open invitation for skunks. Stack lumber and woodpiles neatly to take away the temptation for skunks to burrow. **Tip**: If you are trying to get rid of a skunk, close off any holes allowing them access to their den.

Solutions 3

Critters that Make Your Skin Crawl!

Feel like something is slithering up your leg? You will after you read this.

- **Silverfish**: To reduce the chances of silverfish in the home, remove old stacks of newspapers, magazines, papers, books and fabrics plus food spills and food stored for long periods of time. Often reducing available water and lowering the home's relative humidity with dehumidifiers and fans is helpful. Repair leaking plumbing and eliminate moisture around laundry areas.

- A simple silverfish trap can be made with canning jars, scrubbing them clean and then covering the outside with masking tape to make them easy to climb. These traps are then placed in areas of infestation. The bugs will climb up and fall into the jars and then will not be able to climb the walls to escape. Moist cotton or starchy foods work as bait. Also leave whole cloves where they like to go, they don't like the smell. The next step is to use Diatomaceous earth (dust) used as filter media in swimming pools. If you know someone with a pool, ask them for a cup or visit a near by garden store. If the problem remains call an exterminator!

> *Letter from a contributor in B.C.: About 20 years ago we had a serious infestation of silverfish. I don't remember where I learned this solution, but it worked. A mixture of powdered sugar and boric acid spread in a few places along the baseboards did the trick (take caution around children and pets). No fumigation necessary. I haven't seen a single silverfish since. Submitted by Flora*

- **Bedbugs**: According to Lincoln at Poulin's Pest Control Supplies, "These little critters are on the rise." Bedbugs are small wingless insects that feed solely upon the blood of warm-blooded mammals. If you have small bites on your arms, neck, or shoulders, in addition to spots of blood on the mattress or pillows, you may have a bedbug infestation. Check the mattress for a nest (bedbugs are larger than fleas). Vacuum bed, wash pillows, blankets, sheets and apply diatomaceous earth (heavy bedbug infestations may need more than a second treatment). If the problem remains, call an exterminator!
  Tip: Bedbugs can attach themselves to clothing and other fabrics separate from the bed. Be persistent!

- **Ground Beetles**: Ground beetles are typically an outdoor pest who occasionally move in without paying the mortgage. Homeowners may confuse these beetles with cockroaches, carpet beetles and wood-boring beetles or other household pests. Sealing the home helps prevent ground beetles from entering. If handled, some large beetles will pinch fingers with their strong mandibles (jaws) and emit noxious defensive odors. Use pesticides with care. Warning: Apply pesticides only to plants, animals or sites listed on the label. When mixing and applying pesticides, follow all label precautions to protect yourself and others around you. If pesticides are spilled on skin or clothing, remove clothing and wash skin thoroughly. Store pesticides in their original containers and keep them out of the reach of children, pets and livestock.

- **Larder Beetles**: This species are common throughout the world and play an important role when it comes to recycling. Black larder beetles feed on any dead animal. They are small and dark little critters. Use larder beetle traps to treat as large of an area as possible especially if the traps are showing black larder beetles to be active somewhere you never expected.

- **Carpet Beetles**: The larval stages cause damage to a variety of material. Their preferred food varies with the species, but all carpet beetle larvae can feed on wool carpets and other wool products, furs, hides, horns, feathers, hair and silk. Use traps or pesticide.

- **Lady Bugs**: Although essential to our environment, most people don't like them in the home. Vacuum up successful invaders, or resort to using a spray bottle filled with water and a small amount of liquid laundry detergent. Spray directly onto the ladybugs to exterminate them (or just carry them outside).

- **German Cockroaches**: Seen as tan to light brown, with two dark parallel streaks running from the head to the base of the wings. They have wings but can't fly. This is one of the most common and prominent household cockroaches in the world and can be found throughout many human settlements in the world. Catnip is a natural repellent to cockroaches or kill cockroaches by mixing equal parts sugar and baking powder. Sugar attracts these creatures and baking powder kills them.

- **Dust Mites**: Cover mattress and pillows with laminated covers that reduce penetration of dust mites. Avoid fabric-covered headboards. Cover heating ducts with a filter that can trap tiny dust particles smaller than 10 microns. Wash bedding at 131°F (55°C) or higher. Detergents and commercial laundry products have no effect on mites unless the water temperature is high. Vacuum mattresses and furniture regularly.

- **Pantry Pests**: Rice weevils, granary weevils, grain moths, grain bores, drugstore beetles, tobacco beetle, Indian meal moth, confused flour beetle and red flour beetles are examples of insects that can be brought into homes in packaged foods (although they may enter from outside sources or from adjacent apartments). Often the first indication of the infestation is the appearance of small moths flying around or beetles in or near the food package. By the way, the presence of these creatures in the home does not necessarily reflect on the quality of the housekeeper.

- **Discourage Bugs in Food**: Do not mix old and new foods; if the old material is infested the pest will quickly invade the new. Clean old containers before filling them with fresh food, they may be contaminated and cause a new infestation. Store bulk materials, such as pet foods, in containers with tight-fitting lids.

- **Raccoons**: Discourage raccoons from invading your trash by placing a waterproof radio near trash cans. Set the station to a "talk" station, the voices will discourage raccoons from the area.

- **Rabbits**: Rabbits are adorable but love to eat vegetables. Visit your local hair salon and collect a bag full of human hair. Sprinkle it around garden plants to keep rabbits away. **Note**: Blood meal, turkey manure and marigolds have proven to be effective rabbit deterrents.

- **Bats**: Build your very own bat house. Despite their creepy reputation, bats make excellent neighbors. They are quiet and polite and they can help eliminate all kinds of pesky insects. A little brown bat can gobble as many as 500 mosquitoes in just one hour!

- **Dragonflies**: Adult dragonflies eat many of the most annoying garden pests so they are a welcome addition to any garden. Even if you don't have a garden pond, a shallow pan of water or a birdbath should be enough to attract dragonflies to your yard and no garden big or small should be without them!

- **Slugs**: To keep slugs from invading your yard, scoop the inside of a melon out (half) and leave it face down near the problem area. In the morning it should be full of slugs; empty them into a garbage bag. Another option to deter slugs is to sprinkle cornmeal in the garden.

- **Termites**: To keep termites from eating your wooden fence posts, pour a little used motor oil at the base of them from time to time.

- **Mice**: Discourage mice from visiting areas around the home, car or barn by shaving several bars of Irish Spring soap and sprinkling them wherever mice tend to gather. **Tip**: Discourage rats and mice with the help of a weasel. They'll soon be gone.

- **Moles**: Deter moles in the yard by mixing ½ cup (125 mL) castor oil with 2 gallons (8 L) water. Pour mixture down the hole; this will not hurt moles but keeps them at bay.

- **Wasps**: Trying to enjoy supper outside but the wasps are buzzing in your ears? Fill a container with dish soap and Mountain Dew. Place the container away from the seating area and watch those wasps disappear. Or, boil 2 oz. (56 g) sugar and a little water in a pan to make a sticky liquid. Pour this into an empty jar or dish and leave in the open where wasps will be attracted to sweetness. They enter into the liquid to feed and can't get out.

- **Fleas**: Eliminate fleas on dogs by adding a few drops of dish soap to your dog's bath. Shampoo your pet thoroughly. Rinse well to avoid skin irritations. **Tip**: Rub bites on a human with a raw onion.

- Citrus is a natural flea deterrent. Pour 1 cup (250 mL) boiling water over a sliced lemon. Include the lemon skin, scored to release more citrus oil. Let this mixture soak overnight and sponge on your dog to kill fleas instantly.

- **Spiders**: To keep spiders out of kitchen cupboards, place whole cloves in a small container like a bottle cap and place towards back of shelf. All insects hate the smell of cloves. This also keeps your cupboards nice and spicy.

- **Gophers**: Make little flags and stick one flag into each tunnel, the vibration keeps gophers out. They do not use tunnels with something in them. Funny how something so simple works so well – give it a try!

Solutions 3

Dear Reena,

I bought a book at a garage sale and put it on my bed next to my pillow. I discovered all these white little sacks in them and all of a sudden I am inundated with bedbugs. It is so bad I had to abandon the bedroom. What can I do to get rid of them? Gordon in Vancouver

Hi Gordon,

You have no time to waste! The adult bedbug is brown to reddish-brown, oval-shaped, flattened and about ¼-⅜" (1-1.6 cm) long; they also have a distinct smell. Inspect all areas of the room using a bright flashlight and a magnifying glass. Remember that the bedbug's flat shape and small body enable it to hide easily in cracks and crevices. Bedbugs, eggs and fecal deposits will go unnoticed with just a casual inspection.

Now, for the full inspection you should leave nothing unturned, no site should be ignored. Check wall sconces, behind electrical switch plates, behind wall posters and between books and magazines on shelves and in racks. Be prepared to inspect all the places near sleeping areas, which may mean taking the bed frames apart.

First step, vacuuming, can successfully remove both bugs and eggs from the surface of mattresses, walls and carpets, especially if you act fast. Close attention should be paid to seams, edges and any crevices. Dispose of the vacuum contents in a sealed trash bag. Steam cleaning can kill some of the bugs and eggs in the carpet that vacuuming may have missed.

Secondly, if evidence of bedbugs is still apparent, apply residual liquid, aerosol or dust residual insecticides such as Demand CS, CB D Force Aerosol and Dri-one Dust. Most likely, you will need to treat 3-4 times in a space of a couple months, as you cut the cycle.

Third, if evidence of bedbugs is STILL apparent, call for professional assistance and pest control.

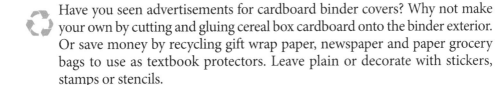

End of Summer Signals Back to School

When the times comes, refer to these tricks & tips to keep your family organized.

 Stuck on You Glue Recipe: Mix ¾ cup (175 mL) water, 2 tbsp. (30 mL) corn syrup and 1 tsp. (5 mL) white vinegar in a pot. Bring to a boil. In a separate bowl combine ½ cup (125 mL) cornstarch and ¾ cup (175 mL) cold water. While stirring, slowly add the cornstarch mixture to the vinegar mixture. Let sit overnight and use.

 Lick'em and Stick'em Stickers: Combine 1 tbsp. (15 mL) Jell-O with 2 tbsp. (30 mL) boiling water, stir until dissolved. Paint on back of pre-cut paper shapes. When dry lick the stickers and apply. Great birthday party project!

 Gruesome Gluesome Recipe: Jazz up plain old white glue by adding various flavors of Kool-Aid packets into approximately ¼ cup (60 mL) cup of glue. Mix thoroughly with paint brushes and watch amazing, fragrant, glossy colors come through.

- Mend torn book pages by placing a piece of waxed paper beneath the tear. Carefully line up the borders of the tear and brush clear drying white glue over the area. Cover the mended area with a sheet of onion skin paper (very thin paper that can be found in most office supply stores) and rub your finger over the area using gentle pressure. Place a weight over the repaired page. After the glue has dried completely, remove the waxed paper and carefully peal off the onion skin. Your newly repaired page should look as good as new.

- Keep homework organized by using a color code system. Assign a special color to each of your courses. When purchasing supplies, keep the color codes in mind. Buy colored folders, notebooks, highlighters and sticky notes that you'll use exclusively for each specific subject.

Have you seen advertisements for cardboard binder covers? Why not make your own by cutting and gluing cereal box cardboard onto the binder exterior. Or save money by recycling gift wrap paper, newspaper and paper grocery bags to use as textbook protectors. Leave plain or decorate with stickers, stamps or stencils.

- Do your kids think they need a new lunchbox and backpack each year? Ummm-no. Unless what they have is really falling apart they can use it a little while longer. Disney characters and celebrity stuff is great for a few months but gets old fast. Save some coin and invest in good quality generic lunchboxes and backpacks or look for backpacks and lunchboxes at consignment shops and garage sales.

- It's one of the universal truths of parenthood: pencil cases, folders, markers and other school supplies are forever disappearing. You may be able to lessen the losses, however, by affixing address labels with a piece of transparent tape to the contents of your child's desk and backpack stuff.

- Do your kids have trouble keeping track of their school pencils, pens and rulers? Puncture three holes along the bottom edge of a sealable freezer bag so it will fit in a three-ring binder to store school supplies.

- For painting crafts, use an empty egg carton to place different paint colors into egg cups or holders, when finished dispose of carton, no mess to clean!

- Little Orwin proudly hands you the pencil drawing that he made at school. You want to protect the drawing against smudges, what should you do? Lightly spray the picture with hairspray so that it will remain intact.

- Create your own finger paint by combining yogurt with food coloring or powdered drink mix. The texture is perfect and clean up is lickity split.

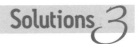

Get Organized for Winter

"Order is the sanity of the mind, the health of the body, the peace of the city, the security of the state. Like beams in a house or bones to a body, so is order to all things." *Robert Southey*

- Before getting organized for winter, ask yourself the following questions: What do you really need to store near the door? What things do you need to have accessible as you walk out the door? What items do you use only occasionally or seasonally that might be stored elsewhere? **Tip**: To keep track of which key opens which lock, trace the outline of each key on an index card and write down which lock it fits. File the cards away for future reference. You can even tape keys you're not using to the correct card and store them until you need them. Speaking of keys, here's **another Tip**: Color code keys to make it easier to grab the right one. Lay keys flat and apply a thick coat of different nail polish shades to the top of each key.

- Gloves or mittens are best kept at point of use. Plus, always keep an extra pair of gloves or mittens permanently in your car glove box (hence the name). Even if you don't wear these gloves often, if you need to change a flat tire you'll be thankful you have them.

- When you find gloves on clearance, purchase more than one pair. When one glove is lost you can re-use the other glove by pairing it with a matching new glove instead of throwing the unmatched glove away (works great for families with kids).

- To avoid children from losing their gloves and hats, stick adhesive-backed Velcro strips along the back of the door to provide a fun place for little ones to stick gloves and hats upon returning home.

- Your shoes will stay clean and shaped if you save all of your shoe boxes and cut one end out of each box. Place your shoes in the boxes and stack.

- Keep a cloth coated with petroleum jelly in a sealed container at your front and back door. Every time you go in or out, give your boots a light rub with the cloth to remove salt marks and preserve leather.

- Tired of searching for mittens and gloves? Use clothespins to secure each pair together. **Tip**: Safety pins work in the same way for extended storage periods.

- My favorite organizing tip for jackets, scarves, shoes, etc. is lockers. If you are handy and you have the space, build yourself a locker room and designate one locker for each member of the family. For smaller spaces, wooden or plastic cubbies will also do the trick.

Solutions 3

Here is an easy solution for storing extra mittens, toques and small winter scarves: Simply roll them or fold them to fit into a clean, empty chip tube containers. Use a permanent marker or a label on the lid to write down what is inside the container. The chip tubes can stand inside a storage bench or lay horizontally on a closet shelf.

- Reduce the amount of storage space needed by keeping your winter gear contained. Large plastic storage containers are easy to find in any discount store and are a great way to keep all of your winter goods in one place. If all of your items have been cleaned, everything can be stored together, including footwear.

- Purchase a tower of baskets for the entrance so that each member of the family has a basket to put their hats and mitts in. Also, install coat hooks, one for each child's backpack and jacket.

- Buy a narrow, plastic drawer unit with wheels on the bottom. Label each drawer with family members' names and store their warm wear in their individual drawer all year. No lost mittens, no last-minute searching for the right hat.

- Sometimes the little nylon jacket hook inside your outdoor garment breaks. No need to fear, key chain rings sewn into the collar of coat's and jackets provide stronger hangers.

- Have furs (artificial or real) cleaned before long-term storage. During the winter months, dust particles sift down through the strands and settle onto the base where they absorb the natural oils and hasten the skin drying and cracking.

- To dry the inside of winter boots in a hurry, use a hair dryer or a shop vac. Put the hose inside of the boot and turn on the blower.

- To remove damp and musty odors in closets, place used coffee grounds in an open container in the area.

- If you need to scrape your windshield but aren't getting a good grip on the scraper with your gloves on and don't want to freeze your fingers, find an old or cheap pair of mitts. Cut a hole in the top just big enough near and just in front of the middle finger. Slip the handle of the scraper through so it's now inside the mitt. Voila! Grip and warmth! *Submitted by Rekha Malaviya*

Don't throw away that old shower curtain! During the winter, cover your car windshield with a section of the curtain (cut to fit) and secure with magnets. This isn't practical when there are howling winds but works well in balmier weather.

Dust off Your Winter Blues

Dust happens. As soon as you dust your furniture, more and more dust collects. But don't give up; the dust war is on! Why? Because dust makes a house dirty and creates problems, from eye irritation to lingering colds and allergies to that annoying itchy nose.

- A large percentage of the dirt in homes is created by the feet (and paws) of the people (and animals) walking through the door. The right kind of mats placed inside and out of all entrances will help cut down on cleaning time. Choose commercial mats like those at the entrances of hospitals and supermarkets (available at janitorial supply stores). Walk-off mats (they give the dirt a chance to be walked off before it gets in) are usually nylon or olefin with a rubber or vinyl back for inside the door and rubber or vinyl-backed synthetic turf for outside on the step. To do a good job, both the inside and outside mats should be four strides long. Vacuum mats regularly or shake them outside. Hose them down and scrub with an all-purpose cleaner as needed. Hang mats until completely dry so that no moisture is trapped under the vinyl backing.

- In most homes, carpet is by far the biggest dust reservoir. It's a huge source of fibers and absorbs dust like a giant sponge. Cut down on dust by vacuuming regularly: behind couches, under tables and obviously throughout all large open areas. Vacuum pathways and busy areas at least once a week. Beat area rugs with a broom by draping them over a fence or clothesline. Smaller rugs should be taken outside and shaken once a week.

- The time has come to dust your ceiling fan blades. Consider using a special dusting brush that stores sell for just a few bucks. A ceiling fan duster usually has a telescoping pole handle, the extension is so you can reach the fan from the floor. It also has 2 soft fabric paint roller shaped style brushes on the end that slide over each side of the blade at the same time. Feeling a little wild? Purchase a dust sweeper with an attached dust catcher that automatically catches the dust as it falls. Carefully shake off the duster outside or rinse the brush clean after each use.

- Next time you clean the fan blades apply a thin coat of floor wax to them. It will keep future dust from settling.

- Consider draping slipcovers over upholstery; this allows you to shake out (or wash) a slipcover as opposed to trying to vacuum dust from an entire piece of furniture.

- In your closet, use an old pillowcase to cover your best clothing to keep the dust off. King-size pillowcases work well when traveling as garment protectors.

- Brush your pets often to reduce shedding. Pet owners will see that much dust and debris can come from pets. Brushing not only gives you quality time with your pet, but reduces the amount of dander and shedding that you end up dusting away.

 Hair and pet brushes can be cleaned by removing excess fur; then soaking the brushes in a sink full of warm water with 2 tbsp. (30 mL) baking soda and 2 tbsp. (30 mL) hydrogen peroxide. Leave for 5 minutes; rinse and dry.

- Keep a paint brush on hand to help out with the dusting. A paint brush is perfect to get in crevices and get the dust out. A stencil brush is handy when the paint brush doesn't do the best job. It is a little stiffer and seems to work better to get dust out of some places.

Dust is a nuisance, but greasy dust is the worst, i.e. the kind found on a range hood or on the top of a kitchen ceiling fan. Regular, full strength liquid glycerin is the answer. Put glycerin on a soft cloth and wipe away the grime. Rinse off with white vinegar.

To remove fingerprints on wood furniture, shake a little cornstarch on the surface and polish with a soft cloth.

- Check and maintain your air filters to make sure they are functioning properly. Air filters will last between 1-3 months, but should be changed as they become clogged with dirt and debris.

- Keep vacuum bags, filters, seals and gaskets in good repair to prevent fine dust from being blown back into the air as you vacuum.

- To replace full vacuum bags, spray the open hole of the bag with water. Place the vacuum bag inside a grocery bag. The water sprayed will reduce the flying dust mess.

Polish teak furniture by applying coconut or olive oil onto a cloth and wiping wood along the grain. Remove any excess.

- Dirt on glass attracts more dirt. Exterior window surfaces should be cleaned often because dirt left over time becomes harder to remove and some types can etch the glass, causing permanent damage.

- To clean and dust tarnished brass, begin by determining if what you think is brass really is brass. Hold a magnet onto the "brass" area, if it clings you are dealing with brass plated metal. There are two types of brass, one is coated with a clear lacquer and the other is not. Clean coated brass by wiping it with a damp cloth. If the lacquer coating is worn or chipped, that area will start to tarnish. Strip off the old lacquer finish and clean the surface, then re-apply a new coat of lacquer. When you lacquer, make sure the surface remains dust free. Hardware stores carry lacquer spray finishes (you can also use lacquer in a can and apply it with cotton balls). Brass that has no lacquer finish on it can be cleaned with ketchup.

 Speaking of dust (another kind of dust): Dusting baking pans with flour can be messy. Fill a salt shaker with flour and use to dust baking sheets. You can also fill a salt shaker with flour for sprinkling onto chicken. Icing sugar can be put in a salt shaker for muffins and the tops of cakes. Or, put cinnamon and sugar in a salt shaker for sprinkling on toast.

An easy and safe way to store Christmas decorations is to cut holes on opposite ends of the inside of a cardboard box. Tie a string from one end inside the box to the other and secure string in holes. Hang decorations on strings and close lid. *Submitted by Peter Fast*

Household Repairs that Will Reduce, Reuse and Recycle

A household disaster can strike at any time. Instead of running to the store to purchase brand new products, why not fix what you already own?

- **DVD Scratches**: You need quiet time so you pop a DVD into the machine for little Dorian but the movie won't work because it has a scratch on it. You have nothing to lose by boiling the DVD in water for 5 minutes. Cool and wipe with white vinegar; 8 times out of 10 the movie will once again play.

- **Stained Lamp Shade**: Depending on the fabric, gently wipe the area with dish soap and water. Or, rub an art gum eraser over the spot. If the stain remains consider recovering the shade with adhesive fabric spray and fabric to match the décor. **Tip**: When recovering lampshades for a bedroom, cut up fabric from pillow shams if they aren't being used – the shades will match the bedding.

- **Elastics**: Broken elastic bands can be a nuisance when they are not strong enough for the job. Get tough by purchasing a package of fabric encased hair elastics; they are reinforced, much softer and stronger.

- **Mildewed Books**: Don't let mildew-plagued books bring down your spirits. Wipe off bindings and pages gently with a clean, soft cloth dampened with the slightest amount of rubbing alcohol (not enough to smear the ink). Next fan out the pages to dry. Alternatively, sprinkle corn flour on each page, leave for a few hours; brush gently.

- **Dirty Leather Book Bindings**: Use saddle soap or petroleum jelly; apply sparingly and gently with your fingers or a soft cloth. Leave for several hours and then repeat.

- **Repair a Leaky Faucet ASAP**. According to the United Nations, there are currently 400 million people worldwide facing severe water shortages. Every bit helps!

- **Broken Lipstick**: Swivel the tube up as high as it will go. Heat the lipstick in the tube using a lighter. Replace the broken section onto the lipstick in the tube. Press and leave in the fridge for one hour to set.

- **Clogged Spray Bottle**: Certain spray bottles have a high tendency to clog. If the top is not made for removal you are best off not to force the issue. Hold the nozzle under warm running water, then remove the residue with toothpicks, gently scrape away any debris that is lodged in the hole. Soak the sprayer in vinegar for a few hours. Poke a hole with a pin or toothpick once again. Also try blowing air through the hole. Or scrub the spray nozzle hole with dish soap and an old toothbrush. **Tip**: Another common spray bottle complaint is that the liquid in the bottle is not full enough to reach the hose. When this happens, place marbles in the bottom of the spray bottle to raise the liquid level and reduce waste.

- **Frayed Shoelace**: Apply clear (or color) fingernail polish to cure frayed ends. Let some of the polish work into the lace for a very firm end. They'll never fray again.

- **Broken Heel on a Dress Shoe**: Best solution is to repair the heel with shoe nails. In a pinch, fix with strong glue such as: Super glue, shoe glue, Krazy Glue or Elmer Carpenter's Wood Glue. Be liberal with it, but don't use so much that the shoe becomes unbalanced.

- **Noisy Ceiling Fan**: A rattling ceiling fan is often caused by a moving glass light fixture and can be prevented with a rubber band. To stop the noise, stretch elastic around the neck where the screws go in.

- **Tearing Sandpaper**: Back sandpaper with duct tape before applying it to vibrating sanders, it will last up to 5 times longer. *Submitted by Denis Joyce*

- **Ironing Board Cover Tear**: When your ironing board ends up with a tear don't despair; simply purchase an adhesive pant patch and iron it over the hole.

- **Thread-less Screws**: Have you ever come across a screw that you just could not get to go in? Try rolling the threads of the screw across a normal bar of soap. It will make the screw go in with ease. *Submitted by Len Huska*

- **Small Nails**: The best way to hammer a small nail into the wall is to use a small comb to hold the nail.

- **Foggy Visor**: There are solutions to keep visors on sportswear helmets from fogging up, e.g. toothpaste or baby shampoo. These solutions are effective but not long lasting. FogTech (fogtech.ca) is a product specifically designed for this conundrum and has longer lasting results.

- Cereal boxes make handy clipboards. Cut the fronts and backs off the box and write your grocery list on them. Your list will be sturdy enough to sit in your grocery cart and you can clip your coupons onto the cardboard.

Solutions 3

Sticky Solutions

- Remove a stuck ring by greasing your ring with butter or oil. Wrap the entire finger with plastic wrap. Pull off the plastic wrap and ring; they should both slide off with ease. **Tip**: Glass cleaner sprayed onto the area is another trick for removing a stuck ring.

- To remove glue stuck on fingers, pour the hottest water that you can stand onto the area and wipe. *Submitted by Don Owen*

- Use Elmer's glue to remove splinters. Pour a small amount over area, let dry and peel. *Submitted by Angie Andrews*

- "Un-gum me you fool!" Remove sticky labels on jeans by wiping the area with rubbing alcohol and gently scraping with a plastic putty knife. *Submitted by Tracia S.*

- Yesterday, my daughter got gum in her hair and I was dreading the "peanut butter" treatment! Rather than use ice or cut her hair; I took the section of hair that was full of gum and put a paper towel behind it, sprayed it thoroughly with cooking spray, let it sit for a couple of minutes and was able to comb all of the gum out. A quick hair shampoo and problem solved! The paper towel was used to help catch the spray from soaking into the rest of her hair. *Submitted by Tina Sawchuk*

- You can use silly putty to clean your computer keyboard. It can also be used to remove lint from clothes.

- Little Himrich dropped his gum on the couch, what should you do? Reach for the duct tape; apply it to the area and pull.

- Glue or staple leftover wallpaper onto cardboard boxes to make attractive storage containers for closets and shelves.

Big Measuring Hints to Size up Your Home

"The measure of life is not its duration, but its donation." Peter Marshall

- Anything can be used as a reference for measuring. For instance, a dollar bill is roughly 6" (15 cm) long. Folded in half, it is roughly 3" (7.5 cm) long. Knowing the measurements of common household objects will come in handy.

- Floor length draperies should be sized ½" (1.25 cm) above the floor, or just short of the carpet pile. Place a piece of cardboard on top of the carpet for an even measurement.

- To measure for custom picture frames, measure the exact width and height of the outside dimensions (including the mat) of your artwork to the nearest ⅛" (3 mm). Use these dimensions for the size of your frame, acrylic and backing board. **Note:** Frames custom-cut to a fraction of an inch are priced to the next whole inch.

- When measuring carpeting or sheet vinyl, get the longest width and length along the floor. Do not multiply them together. Most carpet and vinyl rolls are 12' (3.7 m) wide. If the room is less than 12' (3.7 m) wide, order a roll of carpet as long as the room, being sure to get enough to go through the doorway. Call a professional installer or measuring agent if the room is more than 12' (3.7 m) wide.

- To measure how much paint to buy for a room, add together the length and width and multiply by 2. This number is the circumference of the room. Next measure the height of the room. Multiply this number by the circumference of the room. This will give you the basic square footage of the room. Measure any windows and doors in the room. Multiply the width and height of each opening and then add them together. Subtract this number from the rooms square feet. Simple as pie!

- When measuring butter or shortening, dip the cup or spoon in hot water first. The grease will slide right off.

- To avoid being left with a greasy measuring cup after measuring shortening, butter, honey, peanut butter or margarine; place plastic wrap into the measuring cup first, then just lift the plastic wrap and shake out the ingredient. Use the plastic to grease pans with butter when baking.

- For those of you who would rather take ten preschoolers shopping then sift flour, this tip is for you. To accurately measure flour without sifting (which is often the difference between cakey and moist brownies), whisk or stir the flour a bit before measuring since flour settles.

- Here is a way to keep a measuring cup from getting dirty: find 2, clear 16 oz. (453 g) plastic cups and a liquid measuring cup. Measure 1 oz. (28 g) water in the measuring cup. Pour it into the large plastic cup. Draw a mark at the water-line with a fine tipped permanent marker. Do the same with as many measurements as you need. Remove the cup of water. Place a clean cup inside your new measuring cup. These disposable liners are poor for the environment but help in a pinch when measuring non-edible products.

- Sometimes markings on measuring spoon or cups become worn off and are difficult to read. When this occurs paint a strip of red nail polish over the measurements. Sand them lightly and the numbers will stand out clearly against the nail polish.

- If you're unsure how much batter your Bundt pan will hold, here is a quick way to measure its capacity. Using a cup for measuring liquids, fill the pan to the brim with water and note how many cups it holds. Use a permanent marker to write the capacity on the outside of the pan. Also, measure the amount of batter to make, so that it is within the capacity of the pan. A general rule of thumb is that a cake pan should be ½-⅔ full of unbaked ingredients.

- Spice up your life with this easy tip to speed up measuring while cooking. Get rid of the lids in spice jars that have holes in them. Keep the lids with holes for spices that you tend to sprinkle instead of measuring, such as paprika.

- Heading out to the lake? In order to measure your freshly caught fish accurately; measure from the most forward point of the head (with the mouth closed), to the farthest tip of the tail (with the tail compressed or squeezed), while the fish is lying on it's side.

- Store cheap measuring cup sets inside bins. One measuring cup in the flour bin, another inside the sugar, icing sugar, etc.

SPEAKING OF MEASUREMENTS …

 Did you know? The biggest animal in the world is the blue whale. It has a heart the size of a car and a tongue as heavy as an elephant.

 Did you know? In the course of a lifetime the average person will grow 6½' (2 m) of nose hair.

Wall-to-Wall Hints for Choosing Carpet

Not all carpets are created equally. Here is a list of tips to help you enjoy the fabrics under your feet.

- When purchasing carpet keep in mind: the tighter the fiber is twisted, the more wear the carpet will withstand. Fiber length is another consideration. With long individual fibers, there will be less shedding. Do the finger test: dig your fingertips into the pile and drag them across the surface. If you can scrape up a bunch of carpet fibers, the staples are too short and your carpet may lose density over time. If very few fibers come loose, that's good: your carpet will retain its body. Also notice how it feels: a poor quality yarn will be coarse, dry and fuzzy.

- Many people think that choosing dark-colored or patterned carpets disguise dirt. However, this is not always the case. Carpet fibers play a larger role in showing dirt than color or design. At the present time nylon is the most popular choice for carpet because it is durable, yet inexpensive, lasts longer than other choices and is the easiest to clean.

- **Wool** is another carpet option, especially for luxury carpets and area rugs. Wool has a higher price point and is more difficult to keep clean while on the other hand, has legendary resiliency and is naturally flame retardant.

- **Polyester** is an exceptionally soft fiber that provides great color clarity. This man-made fiber is stain and fade resistant and less expensive than nylon.

- **Polypropylene (Olefin)** is the fastest growing carpet fiber on the market. It is extremely resistant to stains, fading and moisture. Polypropylene's lower price offers great value for your cash.

- What about **acrylic** carpet? Acrylics have lost popularity since the 1960's broadloom carpet era. While acrylic looks and feels similar to wool it does have a tendency to fuzz and pill.

- Texture and quality of a carpet are determined by its construction and the finish applied to the pile. Before purchasing carpet, test the density by bending the carpet sample back with the pile side towards you. Observe how much of the backing you can see, this will tell you whether the carpet is dense or not. The less of the backing that you can see, the better the quality of the carpet. Always get a sample of what you are ordering; this way you will be able to compare the quality of the carpet that gets delivered to your door. Be aware! Some carpet companies sell you the better grade but deliver a cheaper grade. Don't be fooled. Before the carpet is off the truck, make sure it matches your sample.

- For high traffic areas, consider **Berber**. Though the price may be a little higher than other types of carpeting, Berber is constructed of level loops that are not cut and do not flatten overtime unlike pile carpets. A multi-colored Berber in shades of grey, taupe and cream is a hardworking choice for family areas, blending well with many decors and hiding dirt.

- Use a scrap of extra carpet to line the inside of a tool drawer. Tools will remain in place instead of sliding around.

- Before you vacuum, tape a small paper bag to your belt so you have a place to collect pins, elastics and other miscellaneous items that often interrupt your vacuuming groove (that's right, I said groove).

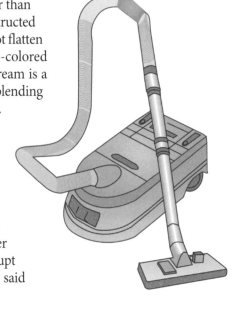

- Save old hairbrushes and use them to clean your vacuum cleaner attachments. The dirt and hair will come off with little effort.

Green Tip: The carpet industry has been innovative in developing sustainable products, carpets, rugs, padding and installation materials with low volatile organic compound (VOC) emissions are now readily available. While various types of nylon, polyester and polyolefins do contribute to pollution (due to extraction of fossil fuels and manufacturing), some of today's fibers have become environmentally sustainable. Before purchasing carpet find out whether the carpet and the package for shipping are recyclable. Also ask if the carpet has been treated with strong chemicals and what kind of glue will be used for installation.

Caring for Hardwood Floors

There are few things more strikingly beautiful than walking into a room with hardwood floors. Floors can set the tone for the entire home.

- Before attempting to repair hardwood floor scratches, determine the type of finish. If the floor has a wax finish the scratch will penetrate all the way into the wood. On the other hand, a floor with a surface finish is recognizable because the scratch will not have penetrated into the wood. A scratched hardwood floor with a surface finish requires a touch-up kit made for urethane finishes. **Tip**: When repairing scratches, work from the outside in.

 Hide tiny scratches on hardwood by spreading peanut butter onto areas. Let sit for 1 hour and wipe off all excess.

- Heel marks on wax finished hardwood can be repaired by rubbing a small amount of wax in with fine steel wool and hand buffing to shine. Also try erasing heel marks with an art eraser.

- Eliminate squeaks in hardwood floors. Begin by determining the exact location of the squeak and locating an adjacent joist below the floorboards by tapping along the floor (this may be difficult if there is a solid sub-floor). To silence a squeak, try applying liquid wax, powdered soap, talcum powder or powdered graphite between floorboards.

- If the floors still squeak, hammer 2" (5 cm) finishing nails through pilot holes near both edges of the board, then hide the holes with matching color putty or wax or call a professional.

- Cleaning hardwood floors with water is not recommended if the finish is damaged because water may penetrate causing further damage to the wood. If the finish is in good condition, a damp mop can be used to wash the floor. A half-dry mop is enough to clean. Rub the floor dry with a clean towel. However, once in awhile, a maintenance coat may be required. Water should be used carefully on floors and should not be allowed to seep into joints. While cleaning oiled hardwood floors, clean with rags moistened in manufacturer recommended cleansing solution.

- Dog saliva stains on hardwood? The stain may be approached by gently rubbing with fine steel wool and applying a wood floor cleaner. Wet the affected area and then sprinkle meat tenderizer on the spots; let soak for a few moments, then wash. Or go to your local antiques mall or woodworking center and find a product called "Howard's Restore-a-Finish", this item is used by professional restorers for all kinds of water damage. It basically penetrates the finish and returns it to a non-cloudy, non-marred finish. For saliva stains that just won't budge you'll have to strip, sand and then re-apply varnish or polyurethane. If the stain still won't come out, call a professional or change the affected boards.

- Pet stains are a particular problem with older floors that have only been waxed. To remove stain, clean the area several times with biodegradeable liquid soap and warm water until yellow is gone. Next pour 3% hydrogen peroxide on the stain and let it sit until it dry. Repeat this process several times until the wood is no longer black. Rub the area with white vinegar to relieve the smell. When you are sure that the smell is gone, re-stain the wood and polyurethane the area. **Tip**: Another product to look for when removing odors from hardwood is Nature's Miracle (available in pet stores).

- Chewing gum or wax on hardwood, yikes. Fill a secure sealable plastic bag with ice cubes and place it over the area. This will cause the wax or gum to harden and become breakable. Use a plastic scraper and gently remove the material. The floor will need to be re-polished.

- Water stains on waxed finished hardwood can often be removed by carefully rubbing the spots with number two steel wool. Soak the steel wool in water and gently wipe.

- Nail polish on hardwood can be tricky. Lacquer thinner will remove nail polish but it will, in some cases remove the floor finish too. Blot the spill with a white rag and small amounts of lacquer thinner; re-finish as necessary.

- Latex paint on hardwood should be cleaned with dish soap, water and a plastic putty knife or "Goof-Off" or paint thinner; re-finish as necessary.

Bloodstains on waxed hardwood floors hydrogen peroxide. Use 50/50 cold water and 3% hydrogen peroxide. Re-wax and buff.

Remember: Some solutions require more than one application in order to be effective. Test all products on an inconspicuous area first!

 Green Tip: Products manufactured from rapidly renewing forests can provide you with a beautiful, affordable, environmentally responsible and durable floor. Bamboo, cork and eucalyptus mature in roughly half the time (or less) that it takes hardwoods, grown in colder climates, to reach market size.

- With such a wide variety of hardwoods available, what works for one floor will not necessarily work for another. If hardwood becomes sticky from cleaning solutions, combine 2-gallons (8 L) warm water, 3 tbsp. (45 mL) household ammonia and ½ tsp. (2 mL) dish soap. Mop the floor to dampen (no need to rinse). Test on an inconspicuous area first.

Important Note: If you are concerned about buying local resources read this letter sent in by Jim of Winnipeg, MB.

"Bamboo, cork and eucalyptus do not grow in Canada; these are products largely from Asia. Our Canadian forest industry is dying with thousands of rural Canadians unable to earn a living and provide for their families. In the past few years, our forest industry has made important changes that make them more environmentally conscious and aware; pine or oak are popular and the loggers have become far more aware of the effects on the environment. We need a vibrant forest industry. Buying woods from other nations does not guarantee environmentally responsible products, in fact it hides from us the damage done to the earth and people in other countries. It's time we Canadians make a greater effort to buy Canadian and support our own."

Solutions 3

Go Green in the Kitchen

Whatever the reasons and goals are, there are more options available today for "greening" your kitchen. Green kitchen design can be eco-friendly without losing luxury and style.

- If you are planning to hire help for a kitchen renovation project, look for contractors who use green products and are familiar with green building techniques.

- The refrigerator is one of the home's highest consumers of energy. Make your fridge and freezer run at their energy-efficient best and prolong their lives by cleaning the condenser once or twice a year so their motors don't have to run as long or often. Purchase approved energy efficient appliances. Once you have "green appliances" use the water and energy-saving settings on the kitchen's refrigerator and dishwasher.

- Increase the efficiency of your refrigerator/freezer by keeping them away from heat sources (direct sunlight, furnace vents and radiators) and other appliances (oven, stove and dishwasher); they will need to work harder to stay cool.

- Want to freeze hamburgers? Save the plastic from individually-wrapped cheese slices and use them between the patties.

- Check the temperature settings; keep your refrigerator temperature between 35°F (1.7°C) and 38°F (3.3°C) and the freezer compartment at 0°F (-18°C) for maximum efficiency and safety.

- Thaw foods in the refrigerator. Because it is already running, it uses less energy than a microwave oven. However, you will have to plan ahead. Don't leave foods out on the counter to thaw; bacteria can develop.

- Small containers of food use less energy to freeze than if food is frozen in larger portions.

- A freezer uses the same amount of electricity to operate no matter how full it is; keeping the freezer full is energy wise.

- Inefficient cooking practices can be a huge energy waster! Keep a lid on pots while bringing to a boil and simmering. Use a toaster oven rather than an electric oven when cooking small items and choose a hand-held blender over a food processor whenever possible. Thaw frozen food completely to save on cooking time and be sure to keep your oven door closed while using. Peeking, causes as much as 20% of the heat to escape – meaning your oven has to work hard to heat itself up again.

- Cook a complete meal in a pressure cooker instead of using several pots and pans. The pressure cooker uses less energy and there's less to clean.

- Turning off the stove before the cooking time is up makes good use of stored heat because the food continues to cook.

Less heat is needed to use the self-clean cycle of your oven if you turn it on after the oven has been used for cooking or baking.

Try using less water when cooking vegetables. You will use less energy and less water means keeping more nutrients in the vegetables.

Filling a slow cooker to half, uses less energy because the heating elements are located in the side of the pot.

Purchase or make your own less toxic, environmentally friendly dish soaps and kitchen cleaners. Many commercial dish soaps and dishwasher detergents are made with non-biodegradable and water-polluting ingredients such as petroleum and phosphates. To "green up" the kitchen choose a dishwashing soap that is plant-based, biodegradable and perfume-free. **Tip**: Skip the bleach and other strong cleaners and replace with "Household Superstars" baking soda and white vinegar (plain old soap and water is effective in killing unwanted bacteria). To get things smelling fresh, add a few drops of all-natural essential oils.

Going green means working with what you already have; think refresh, not necessarily remodel. New paint and updated hardware for cabinets can give you a new look without producing the landfill waste that a remodeling project generates. Most major paint manufacturers now make zero- or low-VOC paint, which means they emit fewer volatile organic compounds. VOCs are linked to health problems and are considered greenhouse gases; the fewer in your home, the better.

Cutting-Edge Cabinets: Cupboards are a major focal point in any kitchen, but many you see today contain a harmful form of formaldehyde. Shop instead for cabinets made of solid wood or wheat board, a material that's typically burned up as waste but can be a great alternative to particle board.

Opt for countertops made from recycled materials such as paper, hemp, glass and aluminum; these are only a few that meet the "reduce, reuse and recycle" standard. Or choose tile, granite, stainless steel or solid wood for your countertop surfaces. Some laminates release undesirable chemicals.

Use reusable, good quality microfiber cloth towels instead of paper towels and clean with earth-friendly water.

Prepare yourself, linoleum is back! Once a staple of the 50s, linoleum is making a come back because of its durability and the fact that it is made from natural and renewable material. Only real linoleum has these benefits. **Note**: People often confuse vinyl flooring with linoleum but it is the real linoleum that is the green choice.

Solutions 3

- A mild dishwashing liquid works well for cleaning cabinet fronts – 1 tbsp. (15 mL) or so in 1 cup (250 mL) warm water should do the job. For trickier bits of food that may be stuck, use a sponge with a green scrubbing pad. Do not to use a scrub brush, steel wool pad or any type of abrasive as these will only scratch the surface of your cabinet. Scouring powder is damaging to cabinets as well. Before drying, sponge with cool, clear water to rinse. **Tip:** Salt is another kitchen cabinet cleanser that is useful as a soak and mild abrasive. It is also known to kill germs.

- To liven up wood cabinets or pantries, wipe them down with a very thin coat of car wax. Dry then buff for a beautiful shine.

- Touchless faucets are making their way into many homes with plumbing manufacturers moving to offer more design options. It's an idea that may seem strange at first, but touchless faucets are actually quite practical, especially for a children's bathroom. They are clearly beneficial in that they limit the spread of bacteria, but they also save water. Consider how much water is wasted while brushing teeth; a touchless faucet ensures that water isn't running the entire time. Combined with a water-saving aerator, touchless faucets can save a substantial amount of water. Also, since the water is set at a specific temperature, having a touchless faucet removes the risk of a child scalding themselves.

- If you've got a sluggish sink and need to unplug it, avoid using chemical drain cleaners. Instead, fill the sink with warm water until it's half full and use a toilet plunger to loosen the blockage.

- Include a recycling center in your kitchen with bins for paper, plastics, glass, metal and organic waste for composting and larger bins in a garage or storage area for collection or delivery.

- Keep your microwave oven clean and you'll keep your energy costs down. Spilled foods absorb the energy used in the cooking process.

- If you need boiling water, use your electric kettle rather than boiling water in a pot on the stove. You use about 40% less energy that way.

- Switch off your coffee maker as soon as coffee is ready; then transfer to a Thermos for the rest of the day.

- Buy a reusable coffee filter instead of using disposable paper ones.

- Cooking for two? Invest in a toaster oven. It uses less energy and can comfortably accommodate meals for one or two.

- If you buy convenience meals for the microwave or oven, many of them include microwave-safe containers that are reusable. Save them and when you make a large meal, make a couple of frozen TV dinners with the leftovers.

Dishwasher Satisfaction

In 1850, Joel Houghton patented a wooden machine with a hand-turned wheel that splashed water on dishes, it was hardly a workable machine, but it was the first patent. In 1886, Josephine Cochran proclaimed in disgust "If nobody else is going to invent a dishwashing machine, I'll do it myself." And she did!

- Before purchasing your next (or first) dishwasher consider capacity: an 18" (46 cm) dishwasher is adequate for 2-3 people and can hold up to 6 or 8 standard place settings. A regular 24" (61 cm) model has the capacity for 12-14 standard place settings and is sufficiently family-sized.

- Look for the lowest EnerGuide rating when shopping for a dishwasher. In 2001, EnerGuide teamed up with ENERGY STAR® to identify the most energy-efficient refrigerators, dishwashers, clothes washers and room air conditioners on the market. The ENERGY STAR® mark identifies products that meet a premium level of energy efficiency. Using the EnerGuide label and ENERGY STAR® symbol to shop for a new appliance is one way to ensure that you'll save money on your monthly energy bills and contribute to helping save the environment from the greenhouse gas emissions and pollutants caused by creating electricity.

- Look for dishwashers with low water consumption. About 80% of the energy required to operate a dishwasher is used to heat water and some models require almost 2 times as much water per cycle as others.

- If you do want higher water heat, look for dishwashers with a booster heater or "sani" setting that brings the temperature of the incoming water up to about 140°F (60°C). This allows you to reduce the temperature of your hot water tank to about 130°F (55°C), significantly reducing your overall water-heating costs. Do not heat water temperatures to higher than manufacturer recommendations'; doing this is an easy way to bring on etching.

- The biggest complaint about dishwashers is dishes not coming out clean. The single most important factor in getting good results is hot water. Remember that water must be at least 130°F (55°C) or higher to work effectively. This is documented by the major manufacturers of detergents, such as Proctor & Gamble. Otherwise, greasy films will occur, along with soap residues left on glassware.

- If you are itching to get your etching under control determine whether the film is removable or permanent. How? Soak an etched glass in undiluted white vinegar for 15 minutes. Or wash the glass with warm water and concentrated dishwasher detergent. Or run a dishwasher cycle of etched dishes with citric acid in the soap dispenser. If the film comes off, it is likely caused by hard water minerals, improper amounts of detergent, or unsuitable water temperature. If it's permanent etching, you can't make it clear again.

- If suddenly your dishes aren't clean, check your water heater's temperature dial to be sure it hasn't been changed recently.

- Also, be sure dishes haven't prevented the detergent dispenser from opening properly during the wash cycles or kept the spray arms from turning, the lower arm from rising, or the spray from reaching the upper rack's dishes.

- Thirdly, during the wash cycle, listen to the spray arm spinning inside. If it seems to be spinning poorly, clean out the spray holes in the spray arm(s) with a stiff piece of wire. Wait for the machine to cool and then remove the spray arm(s) by unscrewing the hub cap and lifting the arm(s) off.

- Gel dishwasher detergent vs. powder: According to a recent survey gel dishwasher detergents are a cause of many dishwasher headaches: Etching is a greater problem when using gels and gel does not work well with hard water and tends not to rinse off of dishwasher interior as well as powdered dishwasher detergent.

Homemade Dishwasher Soap: Mix 50/50 borax and washing soda; use as you would powdered dishwasher detergent. Proportions may be adjusted to avoid film on dishes. Check manufacture notes before using.

- Dishwasher rinse agents help to get your dishes cleaner but they sure are pricey. Fortunately, there's a cheap alternative: Vinegar. **Tip**: Dishwasher looking a bit dirty? Fill the detergent dispenser with vinegar (no detergent at all) and run it through a cycle. This will clean the wash tub, racks and even the heating elements.

- If stains on your stainless steel dishwasher washtub seem permanent after many cleaning attempts, ventilate as much as possible and use "Iron Out" according to the package directions. The stains will soon be a distant memory.

Polish stainless steel dishwasher exteriors with olive oil, it's the best! Pour oil onto a soft cloth and wipe stainless steel along the grain. Remove all excess and leave.

Rinse your dishwasher cutlery basket with ease. Fill it and place it in the sink unrinsed. Spray the entire basket with water to rinse instead of rinsing a few pieces at a time. Return to the dishwasher and wash as usual.

If dishes are left in a dishwasher for any length of time, sprinkle about ½ cup (125 mL) of baking soda over the bottom of the dishwasher. It will help to reduce odor build-up.

- Select the dishwasher's no-heat or air-dry cycle. Turn off the electric element that heats the interior of the unit causing water to evaporate. It is easy to do and will save on your hydro bill.

Scrape off your dishes instead of rinsing them and run the dishwasher only when it is full.

Keep Pots & Pans Shiny

The easiest way to make cookware cleaning a snap is to throw everything away after each use, but since that isn't an option …

- To clean the inside of a burnt stainless steel pot, soak the pot with Coca Cola and leave for 24 hours. Wipe away the burnt mess with stainless steel wool or crumpled up aluminum foil. Be cautious not to scratch the surface, if this occurs food is more likely to stick to the interior during subsequent cooking adventures. **Tip**: Baking soda (or salt) is another option for clean-up but keep in mind, leaving baking soda on aluminum pans for longer than 1 hour can cause pitting, or dark spots, on the surface.

- To clean a badly burnt pan, slice an onion, put it in the pan and add enough water to cover the burnt part. Heat until the water is boiling; remove and leave to cool.

- Muffin tins are time consuming to wash, add to that the extra care needed so that the surface is not damaged and you might as well take the day off of work to clean. An alternate solution to coated bakeware is silicone. This flexible material can be tossed into the dishwasher and needs little to no grease prior to using. Silicone baking/cooking material is becoming available at many retail outlets and comes in a variety of shapes and colors. Kitchen cleanup just got easier!

- Silicone distributes heat evenly, but as with dark metal pans or regular non-stick tins, cakes baked in silicone pans may require less time in the oven. The drawback to silicone cookware is that it bends and twists and therefore care should be taken when removing pans from the oven (a metal pan may be placed underneath).

- Silicone slip-sheets are practical, affordable and extremely easy to clean. Purchase a shiny metal baking pan and cut the silicone slip-sheets to fit the size of any baking pan. After baking is complete, pop the slip-sheet into the dishwasher and sit down with a good book.

- The subject of non-stick cookware continues to be a topic of debate. Non-stick (Teflon) bakeware, if scratched has been found safe by some and unsafe by others. **Tip 1**: When cooking with non-stick pans, low to medium temperatures are recommended. Safety of non-stick cookware is still being researched.
  Tip 2: While stainless steel pans do need to be greased, they are no more difficult to clean than a stainless steel pot.

- **To Clean a Burnt Fondue Pot**: Rinse the pot and drop in a 3-4 tbsp. (45-60 mL) dishwasher detergent and enough hot water to cover the bottom. Let sit for 10 minutes and scrub, being careful not to scratch the pot.

- Cast iron is wonderful for frying just about anything from baking cornbread to searing meat. It is versatile and retains heat for a long time. Once in awhile, give your cast iron pan an intense cleaning by placing the skillet inside a wood stove or on a bon fire pit (at your next cookout). Allow the fire to burn up food (move the pan around so that it does not crack). After you are able to carefully retrieve the pan from the fire, wash the ashes off and re-season the pan. The perfect scenario is to place the pan on very hot coals without a flame. **Tip:** Do not use detergents or dishwasher to clean cast iron as it will destroy seasoning.

- Looking for a pizza pan that will provide a crisp crust? Stoneware is an exciting innovation in cookware and a natural product that seasons itself over time. Do not use soaps or detergents to clean stoneware as it is porous and the soap will seep into the pores, eventually picking up a soapy taste. To clean stoneware, rinse with water, wipe and store. Stoneware is great for meatloaf, bread and much more. **Tip:** In the market for a metal pizza pan? Choose one that is perforated which allows air to flow; the crust will bake from the bottom up and be nice and crisp.

- Glazed ceramic or glass cookware is still a popular choice. Although it does require greasing, it looks brand new time after time. Many of us already own a set of "French White" casserole dishes but check out the latest in colors, textures and sizes of the glass/ceramic baking dishes lining store shelves.

- Clean tough stains on enamel pans by covering the bottom with a layer of water softener salt. Cover with a wet towel and leave for several hours to loosen food.

- Don't throw away lemon peels, put them in a blender with a little water and use the solution to lift out tough grease stains in the kitchen. What a way to save money!

- Clean copper pots and pans by sprinkling them with salt on the dirty areas and then scrubbing with a vinegar-soaked rag. The job is made even easier if you run hot water over the bottom of the pan first. The heat helps the salt and vinegar work effectively. Keep in mind that copper is sensitive to air and oxidizes (tarnishes) faster in moist air.

- It's a good idea to match the size of your pot to the size of your range's element to avoid extra heat going to waste.

- Do you use a gas range? Make it more energy efficient by adjusting the flame so only the bottom of the pot or pan is covered.

Get Organized in the Kitchen

Whether you are organizing the kitchen or preparing food for the family, there's no room in the house as busy as the kitchen, so make the most of what you have!

- Organize meat in the freezer by dividing each product into type: ground beef, chicken, seafood, deli-meat, pork and ham, beef, etc. Put each meat into its own plastic basket labeled with a laminated card. This will make locating supper a snap. Replenish newly bought meat by placing it onto the bottom of the container so that everything is used in the order it was purchased.

- Before plunging into a new recipe, line up all of the ingredients on the counter and remove each lid. Close each lid after it is used, this way you do not need to wonder whether you already added that ingredient to the recipe.

- Keep recipe books looking new by tucking a folded clear plastic bag inside of each recipe book cover. When the time comes, open the book and lay it inside of the plastic bag so that you can see the recipe.

 Clean the kitchen exhaust filter with ½ cup (125 mL) water softener salt and 1 gallon (4.5 L) warm water. Scrub with an old toothbrush. *Submitted by Hannah Barry*

 Potatoes take food stains off fingers. Slice a potato and use the exposed side to rub stained hands, wash as usual. *Submitted by Edna Tan*

- Stop mildew from forming on wooden utensils. Save the "Silica Gel Do Not Eat" packages that come in shoes boxes and pop them into kitchen drawers or storage boxes. Silica packages will absorb moisture and stop mildew.

- If you choose to remove the cabinet doors when painting or refinishing, be sure to label or number the doors so they'll go back in the right place. The holes for the hinges (door and frame) need to match too, so you can easily determine which door goes where.

- Cheese graters can be a hassle to clean. Rub the grater with the pulp side of a lemon and watch the cheese residue come out.

- Clean underneath the fridge by placing a sock onto the end of a measuring stick. Move the stick back and forth on the floor.

Solutions 3

- Squirt liquid dish soap onto your counter sponge (if you keep one by the sink), rinse and squeeze it out, leaving lots of soap in the sponge. Doing this will prevent it from getting sour. *Submitted by Dallas Jonson*

Sponge Cleaner: Soak your sponges in a container of white vinegar overnight. Squeeze them out in the morning and they'll be refreshed and ready for use. Or toss your sponge into the dishwasher every few days to sanitize.

- Whip cream with less mess. Poke the beater ends into a piece of waxed paper large enough to cover the top of the bowl. Whip as normal.

Food coloring on fingers? Dip a wet toothbrush in water and then in baking soda, rub the toothbrush along fingers.

- Did you know that baby oil is a great product for removing grease from hands without resorting to abrasives? Rub a little on your hands before and after each job.

Clean a coffee grinder by blending a piece of stale bread through it. Or drop a handful of uncooked rice into the grinder and grind for a few seconds.

- With proper care and constant use, wooden salad bowls remain beautiful as time goes on. A new salad bowl should be seasoned unless it has a special finish. Season the wood by rubbing it with sweet oils. As the bowl is used, salad oils will continue to season. After each use, a wooden salad bowl should be washed in warm water, rinsed in cool and dried. If the bowl is heavily soiled, clean it with a small amount of denatured alcohol on a cloth or use an abrasive pad. Rewash and re-season the bowl. Store in a dry place away from heat.

- To avoid wet sleeves and arms while washing windows, take a large sponge and make a slit through the middle, slipping it over your wrist. When the sponge becomes wet simply ring the water out and put it back on your wrist.

- Win the fight against tough grease and carbon build-up on barbecue grills with the help of a pumice stone. Apply dish soap and water to the pumice stone and carefully wipe away the grime.

Clean your barbecue grill with newspaper soaked in vinegar. Place the wet newspaper onto the warm (not hot) grill and leave for 1 hour. Wipe and discard paper.

- Here's a zesty idea! No need to cut a lemon in half to extract lemon juice. Instead use fork tines to pierce the skin, squeeze out the required amount, wrap and refrigerate.

Clean a burnt pot by cooking tomato sauce in the same pot. The acid from the sauce helps to lift away stuck-on residue.

 For really tough stains on china cups use one of the following cleaning techniques: wipe the stain with whitening toothpaste, or make a paste of baking soda (or washing soda) and water; scrub. Or put 1 tsp. (5 mL) citric acid and 1 tsp. (5 mL) lemon juice and fill the remainder of the cup with hot water. Leave overnight.

- To have porridge ready and waiting in the morning, measure oats into a Thermos flask the night before. Add the correct amount of boiling water and put on lid.

TRIVIA: WHERE DID THE NAME "LAZY SUSAN" COME FROM?

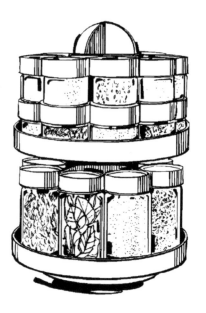

The "Lazy Susan" made its first written appearance in a 1917 Vanity Fair advertisement for a "Revolving Server or lazy Susan". These revolving serving trays have been around since the 1700s, when they were often tiered and called "dumbwaiters." Dumbwaiters were so called because they quietly (hence "dumb") took the place of waiters in the dining room. The theory of how the name changed to "lazy Susan" suggests that servants were often named Susan, so that "Susan" came to be almost a synonym for "servant," and the "lazy Susan" was essentially functioning as a servant who never had to go anywhere (hence "lazy").

Solutions 3

Cut, Mince and Dice Grocery Bills

The average North American spends more than 30% of their monthly budget on food, according to the Economic Research Service, a division of the US Department of Agriculture. Tallied up, that's a national grocery bill of more than $2 trillion annually.

- When possible, consider heading to the grocery store, without the kids. Solo grocery store trips reduce impulse purchases.

- Keep a running list of needed grocery items on the front of your refrigerator. Kids can help with this, i.e. if they used the last of the pancake syrup; having them write it on the list accomplishes two things. First, your grocery list is already made up (except for adding the sale items from flyers) and second, you won't be making another trip to the store later to pick up forgotten items.

- Consider buying frozen seafood such as tilapia, flounder, salmon and shrimp. The price is typically 20-30% less than the fish in the counter that may have come to the grocery on ice or been previously frozen anyway.

- Look to the top and bottoms of grocery store shelves; the most expensive items are positioned at eye level.

- Buy bulk when it makes sense. Foods like oats, rice, dry pasta, legumes and dried fruits can be kept for a long time and are often cheaper when they are sold in bulk. But not all bulk or large-size foods offer huge savings. For example, if extra-large cans of vegetables or fish contain more than your family can eat for a meal, you may end up wasting unused portions.

- When scanning store sale circulars and manufacturer's coupons, most consumers glance at the pictures rather than read the words. What's binding is the wording and more often than not, it says "good" on any. So while you might not be a fan of say, Froot Loops, read the fine print and you'll find that this coupon is good for any other Kellogg brand as well.

- Watch out for signs labeled "SPECIAL;" this word does not necessarily mean that the food is on sale.

- Pre-cut and pre-mixed produce can cost more than double the usual price, so you'll save a bundle by peeling, cutting and mixing at home. And carefully examine the produce on clearance. For example, those slightly soft tomatoes might be perfect for the pasta sauce you'd planned to make later in the week.
  Tip: Pre-grated cheese can cost up to 70% more than a block of cheese.

- Don't go to the grocery store hungry. Eat a meal or snack before you go or you will end up buying more than you had planned. You can even keep snacks such as trail mix or crackers in your car so you can eat a snack on the way.

Don't waste your money on juice boxes for kids. Invest a few dollars in refillable bottles and fill them with juice yourself. **Tip**: Buying juice in concentrate form and mixing with water in a pitcher is always more economical than buying pre-mixed refrigerated juice.

- Purchasing food in jars rather than squeeze bottles will save money.

Cut down on disposable purchases. Use dishcloths and cloth napkins rather than paper towels. Are paper plates really necessary for your barbecue? Why not use your regular dishes? When cleaning your floor, how about using a damp mop rather than a commercial mop that requires a refillable solution?

Buy local. When food doesn't have to travel far, it requires less packaging materials, fewer preservatives and often costs less.

Buy fresh produce instead of canned. Buying loose or "bulk" is another way to reduce trash. Bulk refers to items that are loosely stored in large bins; purchase only the amount you need and scoop the product into a small plastic bag. Tip: Take a shopping bag to the supermarket or buy a "bag for life."

- Buy items that are going to last longer so you do not have to buy them as often. Yes, there will be some items that do not have a long shelf life but try to find those items that do. Some packaging contains harsher chemicals than others.

Say so long to plastic bags. Canadians use approximately 10 billion plastic bags each year. Reducing that number means bringing reusable grocery bags or previously used plastic bags with you to the store. Another alternative is to use cardboard boxes or carry groceries in a laundry basket.

Plastic is a synthetic material that is made from natural gas and oil. We use plastic in some form in our everyday life. A good majority of a household's garbage is made up of plastics. There are many different types of plastics. For example, a soda bottle is made from Polyethylene Terephthalate, or PET or Code 1. These codes can be found by looking at the number in the chasing arrow recycle symbol. Milk jugs are made from High Density Polyethylene, or called HDPE or Code 2. These two types are the most commonly recycled plastics used to make new products. All plastics should be marked with a code. Even though plastics are marked doesn't mean they can be recycled. Most areas recycle plastics type 1 and 2 and some take other types as well.

 Did you know? Shoppers worldwide are using 500 billion to 1 trillion plastic bags per year. This translates to about a million bags every minute across the globe or 150 bags a year for every person on earth and the number is rising.

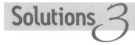

Solutions 3

Food Secrets Revealed

MEAT AND SEAFOOD

- Store breaded cutlets in the refrigerator for one hour before frying to help keep coating in place. Remove cutlets, hold in your palm and press all sides lightly. The breadcrumbs will stay in place and will cook nice and evenly.
- Keep breading on meat during frying by adding ½ tsp. (2 mL) sugar to the batter. *Submitted by Brian P.*
- If your roasted chicken often tends to emerge from the oven dry, stuff an apple inside the bird before placing it in the roasting pan. When it's done cooking, toss the fruit into the compost.
- Juice from canned peaches, apricots or pears may be mixed with melted butter and lemon juice and used as a yummy baste for broiled chicken.
- To get truly golden-brown and crispy chicken you'll need a cast iron skillet. Cast iron simply cannot be beat for even heat distribution and temperature maintenance.
- The important factors contributing to perfect fried chicken are the temperature of the oil and the actual step of frying. Vegetable shortening, lard and peanut oil are all popular frying mediums as they have a high smoke point.
- When barbecuing hamburgers this summer don't press down on the meat when the burgers are on the grill. That will just press out moisture and you'll end up with dry burgers.
- Before barbecuing shrimp, thread them onto two skewers instead of one; this keeps the shrimp from spinning around when you turn them on the grill.
- Reduce the fat content of cooked crumbled ground beef in sauces or casseroles by rinsing after browning and before adding to a recipe. Here's how: Cook meat until done, drain and rinse with hot water. Drain once again and blot dry with paper towels.
- Fried meats can be drained on a brown paper grocery bag. **Extra tidbit**: Because more and more brown paper grocery bags are being made from recycled paper, which contain microscopic bits of metal, don't use them in the microwave. The metal could cause the paper to catch on fire.
- Add 1-2 tsp. (5-10 mL) of vinegar to the cooking water to help tenderize tough stewing meat or braised beef.
- When preparing stuffed ground beef peppers, cut the peppers crosswise instead of lengthwise and leave the seeds in each pepper to add flavor to the beef. This allows each pepper to fit nicely inside a muffin tin before baking. Fill peppers with cooked hamburger meat before baking.

RICE, PASTA AND POTATOES

- Before dropping uncooked spaghetti noodles into a pot of boiling water, grip it firmly with both hands (one on top of the other). Twist both hands in opposite directions and drop pasta into the pot. The pasta will fan out around the edges of the pot and cook evenly.

- Undercook pasta and drain leaving a small amount of water in the pot. Add sauce and freeze. When reheated the pasta will be cooked to perfection.

- Make rice pudding using leftover rice. Place 2 cups (500 mL) cooked rice in a bowl, add 1-2 cups (250-500 mL) low-fat Cool Whip, ½-1 cup (125-250 mL) raisins and add about 2-3 tsp. (10-15 mL) cinnamon. Mix well and cool in fridge until needed. It is delicious! *Submitted by Gail Cathcart*

- Perk up stale potato chips or crackers by spreading them in a single layer onto a microwave safe pan. Heat on high for a few seconds. **Tip:** Stale potato chips and crackers also work well when crushed and sprinkled into casseroles.

- Save foil butter and margarine wrappers to wrap potatoes for baking. They'll be deliciously crunchy.

DAIRY

- Are you tired of drinking white milk? Why not add some oomph to your day by dropping in a bit of red, blue or green food coloring. After all, variety is the spice of life!

- Cheese will not harden as quickly if you butter or oil the exposed cut edges before storing in the refrigerator.

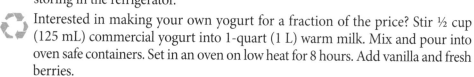 Interested in making your own yogurt for a fraction of the price? Stir ½ cup (125 mL) commercial yogurt into 1-quart (1 L) warm milk. Mix and pour into oven safe containers. Set in an oven on low heat for 8 hours. Add vanilla and fresh berries.

ICE CREAM

- Make your own inexpensive ice cream treats this summer. Choose any ice cream flavor and sandwich it between two graham crackers. Wrap the sandwiches in parchment paper or store in a freezable plastic container. You'll save a bundle!

- Prevent leftover ice cream from becoming gummy and forming crystals. Before shutting the container, press plastic wrap firmly down on the ice cream. This does not allow the air to come into contact with the ice cream, which is what causes the ice crystals and gumming.

- If you purchase ice cream but don't often use it, wrap the container in aluminum foil to prevent ice build-up on ice cream.

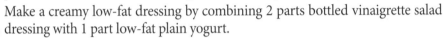
- Messy, messy ice cream. Slip a chocolate chip into the bottom point of the cone to prevent ice cream from dripping out. You can never go wrong with chocolate.

 Chocolate Ice Cream: Stir together 14 oz. (396 mL) Eagle Brand milk and ⅔ cup (150 mL) chocolate syrup. Fold in 2 cups (500 mL) whipped cream. Pour into a foil lined 5x9" (12x23 cm) loaf pan. Cover, freeze and eat.

SALAD DRESSINGS, JAMS AND JELLIES

- Prevent salad dressing from spilling out all over your plate by poking a hole in the protective foil instead of removing it. *Submitted by Darren Dyck*

 Make a creamy low-fat dressing by combining 2 parts bottled vinaigrette salad dressing with 1 part low-fat plain yogurt.

- Transfer your jelly to a small empty plastic squeeze bottle; no more mess, sticky jars or knives! This also works well for homemade salad dressing, sour cream to top tacos or potatoes; good for outdoor dinner parties and is a great way to reuse plastic bottles.

- Do not microwave hardened honey. Granulation is normal and will be accelerated by keeping at cool temperatures. If you wish to make honey liquid, put the glass container in a pot of warm water and gently warm just until it liquefies at about 98.5°F (37°C) or less. Otherwise, the natural benefits of honey will be lost and the flavor tainted. *Submitted by Shirley Richardson*

SAUCES AND GRAVY

Yummy Barbecue Sauce: Combine 2 cups (500 mL) ketchup, 1½ cups (325 mL) brown sugar, ⅓ cup (75 mL) vinegar, 3 tbsp. (45 mL) Worcestershire sauce, ½ tsp. (2 mL) pepper and ½ tsp. (2 mL) salt. Brush onto meat during the last 5 minutes of grilling.

- Give your gravy a boost. To the roaster add 1 onion, 1 garlic clove and several pieces of bacon. Bake contents with meat; remove onion, garlic and bacon just before making gravy. *Submitted by Ken Penner*

- Lumpy gravy got you down? Blend 1 tsp. (5 mL) salt into the flour or cornstarch (depending on what you use) before adding water. **Tip**: Darken and liven up gravy by adding 1 tsp. (5 mL) instant coffee to the roasting pan.

- While cooking tomato sauce, add ½ tsp. (2 mL) instant coffee to the sauce. This extra step takes the acidic edge off of the tomato sauce.

- To fix runny tomato sauce add bread crumbs. The texture and taste will not be a problem and the consistency is a symphony to behold.

- To fix lumpy homemade sauce, stir in chopped garnishes such as olives, lemon zest, pine nuts, sautéed mushrooms, capers, tomatoes, raisins or tiny pieces of carrots and celery. Sprinkle with fresh herbs.

CAKES AND COOKIES

- Have you ever baked a cake that fell in the center? Try different fats or oils in your cake recipes. Too little fat in cake batter makes a cake dry. Too much fat results in a crumbly, heavy cake which may fall in the center.

- One of the key factors when baking a cake is making sure the oven heats to the correct temperature and remains constant. Check oven temperature by baking a white cake at 350°F (180°C) and watch how it bakes. If the temperature is correct it should rise evenly while remaining almost perfectly level on top.

 Frozen concentrate juice cans, make excellent cookie dough molds for refrigerator cookies. Pack the dough in the washed out can. When ready to use, push the dough out from the bottom or slice the can open lengthwise.

- To make perfectly shaped cookies, place the uncooked cookie dough into an empty paper towel roll. The paper towel roll will need to be slit along the center. Place dough inside the tube and close with a rubber band. Refrigerate for 1 hour, open, slice dough and discard paper towel roll. Bake cookies.

- Fill a pastry bag easily by opening it and dropping the bag inside of a tumbler. Fold the empty pastry bag outward so that it drapes over the cup around all sides. Fill the bag with icing.

- If you don't have enough batter to fill all cupcake tins, pour 1 tbsp. (15 mL) of water into the unfilled spots. This helps preserve the life of your pans.

- Prevent freshly baked cookies from turning into cookie crumbs when lifting them off of the pan by loosening them with dental floss. Run a tightly held piece of dental floss under each cookie to raise it from the pan. *Submitted by Tom Plett*

- Add flour to baking sheets to keep cookies from spreading too thinly while baking. *Submitted by Kim Thompson*

- Freeze your pre-shaped cookie dough. Virtually any drop cookie can be easily frozen in its dough state to bake at a later time. Simply line a jelly roll pan with plastic wrap (make sure that the pan fits flat in your freezer), scoop out your dough into balls with a cookie scoop and place each ball, side by side on the pan. Fit as many as you can tightly together. When the pan is full, cover the dough with plastic wrap and place it flat in your freezer. When the balls are completely frozen, lift up on the bottom layer of plastic wrap to release the balls individually; place in a freezable container. Return to freezer.

- If cookie dough gets gluey, resist the impulse to add extra flour so that the cookies don't become tough. Cool in fridge until firm or roll out between two pieces of waxed or parchment paper.

Solutions 3

- For perfectly decorated sugar cookies, cut each cookie with a cookie cutter on the baking sheet. This will prevent the cookie from losing its shape. After removing all excess dough, reposition the cookie cutter onto the cookie and add sprinkles. The cookie cutter is used to keep sprinkles evenly distributed in the center of each cookie. *Submitted by Agnes Darwin*

- Instead of having to ice the sides of a cake, break up Kit Kat chocolate bars lengthwise and stand them up along the outside of the cake.

- To give your cakes a professionally frosted appearance, use a hair dryer set on low to blow the surface dry.

- **Runny Frosting**: Instead of adding more confectioners' sugar, divide the frosting in half and add confectioners sugar to only one, half; you'll have a better chance of thickening the icing.

- Sprinkle homemade cakes with sugar while they are still hot. This keeps them fresh longer. Or put lumps of sugar in with homemade cookies to keep them moist.

- Make decorative sugar cookies by creating a paper stencil. Cut it out and place the exterior portion over the cookie. Sprinkle 1 tsp. (5 mL) colored sugar inside stencil. Remove stencil and bake.

- After freshly baked cookies cool, take 2 uniformly-sized and shaped cookies, place 1 tbsp. (15 mL) frosting on a cookie. Put a Popsicle stick on the cookie like a lollypop stick; place the second cookie on top of the stick and frosting to create a sandwich style cookie popsicle.

- Freeze butter and margarine wrappers; they're handy to use for greasing cake pans, cookie sheets and baking dishes.

- To decorate cakes, fill a clean squeeze-type ketchup or mustard container with icing.

- Spoon dabs of leftover whipped cream onto waxed paper and place in the freezer. When they're frozen, place in a plastic bag and keep in the freezer to use for dessert toppings. Thaw for 10-15 minutes before using.

PIES

 No-Fail Peanut Oil Pastry Recipe: In a large bowl combine 1 cup (250 mL) all-purpose flour and ½ tsp. (2 mL) salt. Beat together ⅓ cup (75 mL) peanut oil and 3 tbsp. (45 mL) cold water with a fork until well-blended. Pour over flour and stir lightly until mixed. Press dough into a smooth ball; flatten slightly. Place between 2, 12" (30 cm) wax paper squares (on a dampened counter top to prevent slipping). Roll pastry until it reaches edges of paper. Peel off top sheet of paper. Invert pastry into the pie plate; then remove the second sheet of paper. Fit the pie crust into the corners of the plate, without stretching, to prevent the shell from shrinking. Use baked or unbaked. **Yields**: One, ⅛" (3 mm) pastry shell. **Caution**: Do not use peanut oil in circumstances where peanut allergies may be an issue.

- To prevent pie crusts from shrinking while baking, lay unbaked pie shell into pie plate, overhang dough ½" (2 cm) over edge. Prick the bottom with a fork. Place aluminum foil inside. Sprinkle dried beans onto foil. Bake; remove foil and beans just before baking time is complete.

- **Even Simpler Pie Crust Technique**: Roll out the pie dough. Fold it to lift it and put it over the bottom side of the pan (the pie plate is on the counter upside down). Trim to fit and poke a few holes in it. When baked, gently remove and put into the pan while still warm and pliable. To make this process easier, put a pan of the same size over the crust and let it fall in place. This will make a perfect crust without shrinking or big bubbles inside. *Submitted by Christine from Cypress River, MB*

- Cut a pie into 5 equal portions. Begin by cutting a "Y" in the pie, next cut the two large pieces in half. You will have five perfect slices. Bon appetite!

SPICES

Did you know? Most of the pepper available to Canadians comes from India. This aromatic, pungent spice is the dried berries of the pepper plant, piper nigrum – black pepper is the whole berry; white pepper the outer skins are removed.

FRUITS AND VEGGIES

- Before putting tomatoes on a pizza, slice them in half and squeeze them over the sink to remove juices so that the tomatoes do not add liquid to the pizza.

- Intensity of tomato sauce may be adjusted by the amount of garlic and crushed peppercorn used. Increase the bite by adding balsamic vinegar.

- To juice a lime fast, stick a fork into the cut part of a lime half and then twist. *Submitted by Pamela Dann*

 Recipe for "**Berrylicious Smoothie**": In a blender, combine 1 cup (250 mL) frozen unsweetened assorted berries, 1 cup (250 mL) pineapple juice, ½ cup (125 mL) fat-free soy milk or 1% milk and ½ cup (125 mL) frozen vanilla yogurt. Blend until smooth.

- Nothing says summer like a gorgeous watermelon filled with fresh fruit. Using a sharp knife, slice a small, thin piece off the bottom of a watermelon (so that the finished basket sits flat on a plate). With the tip of your knife or garnishing tool, score the watermelon in half, horizontally. Mark a strip about 1½-2" (4-5 cm) wide that will form the handle of your basket. Using a small knife, cut around the melon on the lines. A garnishing tool naturally makes V-shaped cuts, which makes the job very easy. Separate the cut sides from the body of the watermelon. If you used a marking pen and there are residual marks leftover, remove them with a new emery board and gently sand them off. With a melon-baller, hollow out the inside of the watermelon. After removing all the edible parts, use a large spoon and gently scrape out the sides of your "basket." Be careful not to scrape too thinly on the handle, as you want it to be stable. Mix the watermelon balls with other ripe, fresh fruits. Use toothpicks to fix the handle on the watermelon. **Tip**: To prevent liquid from filling the basket, cut drainage holes in the bottom of the melon. Be sure to place on a platter with a lip.

- Make leafy vegetables crunchy again. Cut the stem off and separate the stalks. Add ¾ cup (175 mL) granulated sugar to a vessel filled with cold water. Place vegetables inside. Soak for 4 to 5 hours. Drain well; refrigerate.

- Once an onion has been cut in half, rub the leftover side with butter and the onion will stay fresh longer.

- Chop garlic with ease. Place the flat side of a chef's knife on top of the garlic clove, with the blade facing away from you. Holding the handle of the knife with one hand, whack the flat part of the knife with the heel of your other hand to flatten the clove. The peel will slide off.

- When peeling garlic, squeeze the clove to bring out the oil, doing this makes the clove easier to peel. **Extra Tip**: To roast garlic, sprinkle the bulb with a little olive oil, white wine, salt and pepper and wrap it in aluminum foil and roast at 275°F (140°C) for approximately 1 hour.

- To prevent your eyes from tearing when cutting onions, place your cutting board near the exhaust hood over the stove. It pulls the fumes up and away. *Submitted by Grant Burrows*

 Wrap your veggies in a slightly dampened terry facecloth before placing them into the crisper. Facecloths are far more absorbent then paper towels; they are also less expensive because they can be used repeatedly and better for the environment. Or put newspaper on the bottom of the crisper with a few layers of paper towel or facecloth on top to absorb moisture.

- Store celery and lettuce in refrigerator in paper bags instead of plastic bags. Keep the outside leaves and stalks on until ready to use.

- Great flavor! Save celery leaves. Spread them onto paper towels or a paper plate and let them dry. Crumble them into soups, salads and stuffings.

- For crunchier coleslaw, cut a cabbage in half and soak it in salted water for an hour. Drain well and use.

- Create a stunning and edible centerpiece for your next dinner party by displaying veggies in a vase of water. Inside the vessel arrange an assortment of herbs, raw broccoli, cauliflower, long carrots and ribs of celery. **Tip**: Beside the vase set out a bowl of dip for a healthy after school snack.

- Red cabbage will retain its red color during cooking if vinegar or lemon juice is added to the water. The same holds true for blue jeans.

- For best flavor and nutritive value, always cook sweet potatoes whole in their jackets (no scarf or toque required), it takes 35-55 minutes in boiling water and about 35-60 minutes in a hot oven (425°F/220°C).

- Thinly slice unwaxed cucumbers into leftover pickle juice. Refrigerate for three or four days and they will be ready to enjoy.

- Never throw away pickle juice after using all the pickles in a jar. It's great for adding to devilled eggs, coleslaw and potato salad.

Food Brain-Up: Ever wonder what the difference is between green beans and wax beans? Wax beans – because of their waxy yellow color. Green beans are, (well need I say more – they are green) and more common but there is little difference in the nutritional value of the types of beans.

BREAD AND DOUGH

- To keep bread or rolls warm, while the rolls are in the oven, line a bowl with aluminum foil. Remove rolls from oven. To serve, place a napkin over the foil and the bread or rolls inside the napkin. No one will notice, but they will enjoy warm rolls.

- Bread will rise nicely in the microwave if hot bottles of water are positioned in each corner. Cover the dough with a towel and put the bowl into the center of the microwave.

- Help your bread dough rise by placing it in the dishwasher just after you've washed a load of dishes.

- To keep the filling intact when making cinnamon rolls; place a length of dental floss (waxed or un-waxed, not flavored) underneath the roll of dough. Bring the back piece all the way forward and take the front piece to the back, gently pulling both ends until the floss cuts the dough. Much easier than trying to slice with a knife.

- Interested in making healthier bread? Think outside of the bread box by adding rye flour, nuts, wheat germ, parsley, raw grated carrots, yogurt and yeast. Voilà; your bread has now become a healthy treat!

- If your homemade bread is not rising in the oven, it may be due to one of the following reasons: the rising place is too warm or cold, the dough has been allowed to rise too long, water temperature used for dissolving yeast was too cool or too hot, overly stiff dough or dead yeast.

- To grab the full benefits of flax seed in recipes; grind the flax in a coffee grinder. Add ground flax to cereals, muffin and cake recipes. Flax is high in alpha linolenic acid which is a type of plant-derived omega 3 fatty acid, similar to that found in salmon. *Submitted by Angela R.*

- Bruschetta is the original garlic bread and an easy first course for a great Italian meal. When making bruschetta spread butter, mayonnaise or oil onto bread slices as vapor barriers so that the bread does not become soggy before adding toppings. Add toppings just before serving.

- Keep crackers fresh by wrapping them tightly and storing in the refrigerator. *Submitted by Bob Atkins*

- Don't toss out the bread crusts that your family won't eat. Soak them in ⅔ cup (150 mL) buttermilk for 10 minutes. Squeeze out excess milk and add to meatloaf before baking. Moist and yummy! *Submitted by Natalie L.*

- Great stuffing is better then good stuffing! Add a pinch of nutmeg as well as the usual sage or thyme to stuffing for turkey, chicken or goose. If preparing a rice stuffing, give it a crunch by adding ⅓ cup (75 mL) toasted sesame seeds for every 4 cups (1 L) cooked rice. To keep it moist add a peeled, chopped apple.

- Enjoy bread longer when you buy the freshest loaves. Did you know that bread is delivered fresh to the stores 5 days a week? Commercial bakeries color-code each day's production with a different color plastic clip. Always buy the loaf with the twist tie or plastic clip indicating the most recent delivery date. Monday – Blue, Tuesday – Green, Thursday – Red, Friday – White, Saturday – Yellow.

- To eliminate soggy vegetables sandwiches, wrap lettuce and tomatoes separately, instead of adding them directly to the bread. At lunchtime, add them to your sandwich.

COOKING AND BAKING WITH GREASE

- When frying with grease, place a damp towel sprinkled with vinegar on the floor in front of the stove, under your feet. This prevents a greasy floor and makes clean-up a snap. *Submitted by Mrs. D*

- Did you know that when butter is taken out of the refrigerator and put into the microwave, 80% of the aroma and flavor of the butter is lost? Professional chefs store butter at room temperature to soften it. Tip: To soften butter in the microwave for non-baking purposes, select the defrost setting (30% power). Check butter every 5 seconds so that it does not over-soften or melt completely.

- Need soft butter but forgot to take it out of the fridge? Been there. Measure the correct amount of butter and grate it with your cheese grater. Small pieces of butter are easy to work with. Or shave butter with a carrot peeler and shape into roses (that's getting very Martha Stewart).

- Proper disposal of used cooking oil is an important waste-management concern. Oil is lighter than water and tends to spread into thin and broad membranes which hinder the oxygenation of water. A single liter of oil can contaminate as much as 1 million liters of water. Also, oil can congeal on pipes provoking blockages. Therefore, cooking oil should never be dumped down the kitchen sink or toilet bowl. The proper way to dispose of oil, is to put it in a sealed non-recyclable container and discard it with regular garbage.

COFFEE AND TEA

- If your coffee maker produces cloudy coffee, pour 50/50 water and vinegar through the coffee maker to clean it. Next, experiment with a few different brands of coffee. The best coffee flavor is obtained with 6 oz. (170 g) water for every 2 tbsp. (30 mL) ground coffee. If you use less water for the same amount of coffee grounds, you haven't extracted the full coffee flavor from the grounds. If you use more water, you begin extracting too many of the oily substances. If the result of brewing with this ratio is too strong for your taste, simply add a little clear hot water to the pot. Running more water through the grounds will result in coffee that is not only weaker, but also bitter. Finally, run water through a filter, e.g. Brita, before pouring it into the coffee maker. The water you use makes a huge difference.

- When Jan's friends went to Australia for 6 weeks, they visited a tea plantation. The owner of the plantation explained how to remove caffeine from tea. Add hot water to loose leaves and steep for 1 minute. Discard the liquid. This first brew contains most of the caffeine of the tea. Add water to the teapot; let steep for 2-3 minutes and drink that infusion, it has only small amounts of caffeine (over 80% of the caffeine is removed during the first wash). *Submitted by Jan Cooper from B.C.*

MISCELLANEOUS TIPS

- To cure hiccups; cut wedge of a lemon, dip into sugar and eat the lemon. Not only does it taste good, but it also makes hiccups vanish. Or eat a spoonful of peanut butter or Nutella chocolate spread. Or (my favorite) plug your ears and nose and have someone serve you 12 quick sips of water. *Submitted by Kyah Nerbas*

- Another tip to cure hiccups; fill a wide glass with cold water. Put your head over a sink and drink non-stop out of the back of the glass (with your chin inside). It works every time. *Submitted by Pam Stacy*

- When my children had the hiccups, I would suggest "the cure". Which was to mix together vinegar and sugar on a spoon; swallow. Often just the suggestion of "the cure" would instantly stop the hiccups. *Submitted by Julia Hamel*

- Pour flat club soda into house or outdoor plants. The minerals in club soda are beneficial to green plants.

- When I burned my hand with hot butter, I sliced a russet potato, placed the slices over the burn and wrapped my hand with a kitchen towel. The starch in the potato stopped most of the blistering and eased the pain. *Submitted by Pat*

- If you have ever burned your tongue on a hot drink or hot food, you know how much it hurts. Sprinkle sugar on it and the pain will subside.

- White shoe polish will not smear if hairspray is applied to the shoe after it has dried. *Submitted by Darren Mackenzie*

- White shoe polish will have a more even appearance if shoes are wiped with rubbing alcohol before polishing.
- Use a baby bottlebrush dipped in dish soap and water to clean hard to reach places and small crevices in plastic Play Dough toys.
- Line plant and flower pots with coffee filters to prevent soil from dropping through the holes and onto the floor.
- If you have trouble getting a coal or wood fire to burn throw a handful of sugar onto it. The sugar will ignite and help get the fire going.
- Instead of the usual Sunday family dinner, suggest a potluck at your house. Each member of the family is responsible for providing one dish. The variety may not always be a perfect match but the meal is a lot of fun! *Submitted by Sue Schweitzer*
- Use a straight pin to untangle a necklace knot. If the knot won't budge apply several drops of baby oil or mineral oil to the chain, then use the pin to untangle the links. *Submitted by Bertha Stewart*
- Stop paint from dripping outside of the can by punching a few holes on the rim. When the brush is wiped on the edge, the paint will flow back into the can. When the lid is replaced, it covers the holes to prevent the paint from drying out.
- After you finish painting with washable latex paint, wash your brushes and apply hair conditioner to the ends; wipe off any excess with a rag. Bristles will feel as soft as your hair. **Tip**: Speaking of hair, for smoother hair add 1 tsp. (5 mL) baking soda to your regular shampoo and shake (the bottle not yourself).
- Brand new, unused paintbrushes are great for brushing glaze on bread, ham or butter on corn.
- Oops, someone accidentally used permanent marker on a dry erase board. Draw over the mess with dry erase marker and erase as usual. Or apply rubbing alcohol to the area and wipe. Still stuck on? As a last resort dribble nail polish remover onto the board and wipe (test on a small inconspicuous area first).
- Remove permanent marker from countertops and appliances by wiping with rubbing alcohol and a soft cloth. *Submitted by Janice Davidson*
- To open a bottle in a hurry, place a deflated balloon over the cap and twist.
- Rings stuck on fingers will slide off with ease if smeared with Preparation H Hemorrhoid Cream. By the way: Sandra Bullock says that applying hemorrhoid cream around her eyes is her best "secret" defense against crow's feet.
- Rub Chapstick on paper cuts to stop the pain immediately and heal the cut. *Submitted by Rick P.*

UNBELIEVABLY EASY, SAVE-THE-DAY RECIPES!

Have you ever noticed that in general cleaning products do not contain ingredient labels? When products do list chemical names they are unfamiliar to most people. Chances are, **if warning symbols line the container, the product is not good for you or the environment**. Why not try these homemade concoctions instead? No need to go shopping, you probably have everything you need behind your cupboard doors.

- **Grout Cleaner**: Scrub floor grout with Listerine mouthwash and an old toothbrush. **Tip:** For pet messes, allow Listerine to soak area before washing vinyl floors.

- **Toilet Bowl Cleaner**: Sprinkle baking soda around the inside of the toilet bowl. Add a couple drops of liquid castile soap. Scrub with a toilet bowl brush and finish outside surfaces with a damp cloth sprinkled with baking soda.

- **Drain Cleaner**: In a jar combine 2 tbsp. (30 mL) cream of tartar, ¼ cup (60 mL) baking soda and 1 tsp. (5 mL) salt. Drop in drain, chase with boiling water. Repeat as necessary. Or pour ½ cup (125 mL) salt down the drain, followed by boiling water.

- **Scouring Powder**: In a plastic container combine 2 cups (500 mL) baking soda, 2 cups (500 mL) salt and 2 cups (500 mL) borax powder. Store with lid fastened.

- **Coffee Pot Cleaner**: Fill coffee pot with water and 3 tbsp. (45 mL) baking soda. Run water through machine, leave for 2 hours. Scrub with non-abrasive cloth and rinse well.

- **Eye Glass Cleaner**: Begin with a small test on your lenses just to be safe. Fill a spray bottle ¾ full with rubbing alcohol and ¼ full of water. Add a few drops of dish soap. Shake to mix. Spray lenses and gently wipe with a soft cloth (do not use paper towels, toilet paper or tissue).

- **Brick Fireplace Cleaner**: Make bricks easier to clean by applying a finish of penetrating sealer that contains Tung oil. This is moisture resistant and forms a tough coating which can be washed with soap and water.

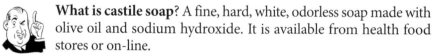

What is castile soap? A fine, hard, white, odorless soap made with olive oil and sodium hydroxide. It is available from health food stores or on-line.

What is sodium hydroxide? The answer is lye, one of the key ingredients used in making soap.

Dishwasher Detergent Recipe: Combine ½ cup (125 mL) liquid castile soap (see note on page 122) with ½ cup (125 mL) water. Stir and add 2 tsp. (10 mL) lemon juice, 4 drops tea tree oil and ¼ cup (60 mL) white vinegar. Blend and store in a squeeze bottle. Use 2 tbsp. (30 mL) per load.

 Window Cleaner: Combine ½ tsp. (2 mL) castile soap (see note on page 122) with 3 tbsp. (45 mL) distilled white vinegar. Wipe with micro fiber drying cloth.

 Liquid Dish Soap: Grate a bar of pure soap into a sauce pan. Cover with water and simmer over low heat until melted. Add 1 tbsp. (15 mL) white vinegar to the water. Pour into a container and use as you would any liquid dishwashing soap.

 Cloth Diaper Whitener: Dissolve ¼ cup (60 mL) baking soda, borax or washing soda in a bucket of warm water; soak for at least an hour. Wash in hot water and homemade laundry soap. Add ½ cup (125 mL) vinegar to the final rinse and let diapers dry in the sun.

 Creamy Soft Scrub: Combine ½ cup (125 mL) baking soda with enough liquid dish soap to make a texture similar to thick cream. Scoop the mixture onto a sponge and scrub. Great for cleaning the bath and shower because it rinses easily and doesn't leave grit. **Note**: To keep the product moist, add 1 tsp. (5 mL) glycerin to the mixture and store in a sealed glass jar, or combine as needed.

 De-scaler: Full-strength vinegar is all you need to clean your kettle and iron. Pour vinegar into the kettle, bring to a boil for 5 minutes. Let cool over night; rinse.

 Shoe Polish: Olive oil with a few drops of lemon juice can be applied to shoes with a thick cotton or terry towel rag. Leave for a few minutes; wipe and buff with a clean, dry rag.

 Rug and Upholstery Cleaner: Sprinkle cornmeal, baking soda or cornstarch on dry rugs and vacuum. Use club soda or soap-based rug shampoo.

 Carpet Steam Cleaner: For people who choose to steam clean their carpets, why not make you own, much less, expensive substitute cleaner? It is not necessary to steam clean your carpets more than once or twice a year. In a large pail, combine ½ cup (125 mL) white vinegar and 3 tsp. (15 mL) clear dishwashing soap. Add enough water to equal 1 gallon (4 L). Test on an inconspicuous area and follow steam cleaner manufacturer's directions.

Lemon Milk Foam Spot Cleaner for Carpets: In a bowl combine ½ cup (125 mL) lemon juice, ¼ tsp. (1 mL) dish soap and 1 tbsp. (15 mL) baking soda. Beat until frothy and drop the foam onto carpet stains. Leave for 15 minutes and blot up foam.

Septic Tank Treatment: Dissolve 2 cups (500 mL) brown sugar and 1 tbsp. (15 mL) bakers yeast in 5 cups (1.25 L) warm water until dissolved. Pour solution into toilet once a month and flush.

Fruit and Veggie Wash Recipe: Simply add 3 tbsp. (45 mL) vinegar to a spray bottle, fill with water. Shake well and spray on veggies, wash as usual, under clean water. Helps to clean fruits and veggies better than ever.

Aluminum Cookware Cleaner: In a dirty aluminum saucepan, combine 2 tbsp. (30 mL) cream of tartar and 1-quart (1 L) water. Bring to a boil and simmer for 10 minutes.

Marble Cleaner: Rub baking soda into the marble with a damp cloth. Then rinse with water, towel dry; and you're done!

Note: If you have leftover toxic cleaning products, take them to a Household Hazardous Waste Collection Site.

Dear Reena,

I bought a plant at a grocery store; it is made of artificial materials like plastics. I am not sure of what the plumes are made of. My son says it smells like dog urine. My sister-in-law, who works at gift shop, says that a lot of their products have similar smells. She likens the smell to a "mouse" smell. I have sprayed it with Febreeze, which is only a temporary fix. The odor seems to come and go. I never smelled it in the store or on my way home from the store. Dorothy

Hi Dorothy: It makes sense that the plant is made of plastic because artificial silk plants are often not silk but rather are made from a variety of synthetic materials and then heat pressed into expertly designed molds. These newer synthetic materials hold shape much better than silk, allowing for a wider range of natural looking leaf and flower designs.

This smelly challenge is similar to that of people who purchase back packs that carry a strange odor. It sounds to me like the culprit is the dye used to color the plant. The not so good news is that any fragrant spray that you use will only be a temporary fix, the good news is that the smell will minimize over time. If your plant is silk instead of synthetic it may still carry an odor, in fact, some experts say "Inferior silk gives off a slight smell of chemicals and silkworm pupa, which will become stronger in more humid and warmer environments."

Since you have observed that the plant is plastic, your best bet is to soak the plant in the bathtub with ½ box of baking soda, water to cover and 3 tbsp. (45 mL) inexpensive shampoo. Rinse and leave outside to dry.

Egg-stra Special Household Hints

The benefits of eggs and egg shells have been known for generations. The larger type eggs such as Ostrich were historically used as water carriers by the hunter gatherer tribes in ancient times.

- After purchasing a carton of eggs, turn the carton over and return them to the refrigerator. This little trick helps eggs last longer.

 In a pinch substitute egg white for glue. Stick light paper together with a little egg white.

- After boiling eggs, don't pour the water down the drain. Instead, let it cool; then water plants with the nutrient-filled water.

- Sometimes a recipe will call for only an egg white or only an egg yolk. Don't throw out the other half! Just freeze it and add it to your next omelet or scrambled eggs. If you make sure they don't get freezer burn, they will last quite a while, but I like to use them as soon as possible.

- When hard-boiling eggs, put a drop of food coloring into the water. When cooked, the eggs can be stored and the color will tell you which are hardboiled.

- When poaching eggs, always add a few drops of white vinegar to the water so that the eggs stay together while cooking.

Bake your eggs in the oven! Remove the crusts of several pieces of bread. Butter both sides and fit them into muffin tins. Drop one egg in each muffin cup onto bread, cover with foil. Bake for about 5 minutes at 325°F (160°C); top with cheese or salsa. Bake for another 3 minutes. Enjoy!

- Never again watch an egg roll off of the counter and onto the floor. Cut egg cartons into three, 4-holed sections, the next time you are baking or cooking you need only take out one section and you don't have to play the balancing act with the eggs. **Tip**: Reuse cartons so that you only cut them once.

 Did you know that egg shells are excellent at cleaning drains? Crush the shells as fine as you can and let them sit in the sink drain basket. Each time the water runs, the egg shells will make their way through to your drain pipes. Egg shells act as a safe abrasive and will help to get rid of any grease or hair buildup. If you use a septic tank for wastes, do not clean your drain with egg shells.

Use paper egg cartons to make little fire starters. Keep one in the laundry room for when you clean out the lint tray. Stuff lint into each section. When full, use old candle stubs and drip wax onto the lint. Store and add to your next outdoor fire.

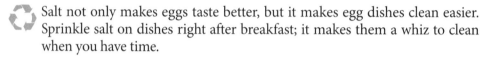

- Store decorative plastic Easter eggs inside of empty egg cartons. Doing this is much more organized then storing them in a plastic bag. They don't get dirty or cracked and can be stacked, boxed and identified easily.

Salt not only makes eggs taste better, but it makes egg dishes clean easier. Sprinkle salt on dishes right after breakfast; it makes them a whiz to clean when you have time.

- **Chef's secret**! When making homemade stock, clarify the final product by beating egg whites to soft peaks, one for each quart/liter of stock. Crumple eggs-shells and mix them through the egg whites. Stir the mixture into the stock and bring it to a simmer, do not let it boil. The egg-whites will coagulate, rise and take any particles or cloudiness out of the stock. Keep a close eye on the simmer (push the coagulated egg-whites to the side a bit to see) and let it simmer for about ten minutes. Remove the pot from the heat and let it sit for another ten minutes. Finally, strain the stock again through cheesecloth.

Unbelievably Easy Egg Drop Soup Recipe (with ingredients that most of us have on hand!): In a soup pot, bring 3 cups (750 mL) chicken broth to a boil. Combine 2 tbsp. (30 mL) cold water with 1 tbsp. (15 mL) cornstarch, stir into boiling broth. Stir 1 tbsp. (15 mL) soup broth into 1 slightly beaten egg. Slowly pour egg mixture into hot broth. Stir constantly until slightly thick. **Tip:** To this yummy delight you can add cooked meatballs, a little soy sauce, Chow Mein noodles or rice.

Egg Stains on Tableware: Use a slice of lemon to rub dried eggs off of cutlery.

- To make a speedy breakfast for the entire family: in a non-stick baking pan, break up eggs; add a little water or milk and whisk. Bake in the oven at 350°F (180°C) until eggs are the desired firmness. Season and serve. Sooo simple!

- Put your grater to good use. Grate hard-boiled eggs for egg salad sandwiches instead of slicing or mashing. What a grate tip!

Ice Breaking Hints

"It's a strange world of language in which skating on thin ice can get you into hot water." *Franklin P. Jones*

- To make crystal clear ice cubes, boil the water first. Let cool and freeze. Boiled water freezes clearly because it contains less oxygen.

- Freezing water into muffin trays will give you giant ice cubes for the punch bowl. If you really want to liven up a party, fill a clean rubber glove with water, tie it and freeze. Just before the guests arrive, remove the glove and place the hand into the punch bowl. Pop a ring into the forth rubber finger if you are planning to propose. **Note**: Food coloring can be an added bonus.

- If you are in a hurry for ice cubes, leave 3 or 4 frozen cubes in a tray and fill the other holes with cold water. The new ice cubes will freeze in half the time. **Note**: Ice cubes are preferred over crushed ice because they melt slower.

- Pre-chill the cooler before packing with food. Fill it with ice then let it cool for about an hour. Replace the ice with fresh ice and pack the cooler with food.

- To water hanging plants or real Christmas trees, place a few ice cubes on the dirt and let them slowly soak into the soil.

- To remove fat from soups, drop in 2 or 3 ice cubes; the fat sticks to the ice cubes and is easy to scoop out.

- Soak a cauliflower head in ice water with the flowerets down to draw out hidden insects. **Tip**: Add 1 tsp. (5 mL) vinegar when cooking cauliflower to prevent discoloration.

- **Iced Coffee**: Brew one pot of coffee and transfer to a carafe. Refrigerate until cold. Fill a glass with ice cubes and pour chilled coffee into glass. Add milk to taste. **Tip**: Stir sweetened condensed milk into warm coffee before pouring it over ice.

- **Edible Ice Flowers**: Fill ice cube tray ½ full with water and freeze. Place one small fresh edible flower on each ice cube. Refreeze. Top the ice cube tray with water and place tray back in freezer.

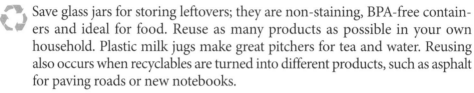

Solutions 3

Reuse, Reduce & Recycle Jars

Did you know that in a two week period North Americans throw out enough glass bottles and jars to fill up what was once the Twin Towers in New York?

Save glass jars for storing leftovers; they are non-staining, BPA-free containers and ideal for food. Reuse as many products as possible in your own household. Plastic milk jugs make great pitchers for tea and water. Reusing also occurs when recyclables are turned into different products, such as asphalt for paving roads or new notebooks.

Keep stews, casseroles, rice, beans and vegetables in clean, glass jars as opposed to plastic containers. Glass jars are safer for heating in the microwave than plastic storage dishes which can leach chemicals into your food. **Tip**: For jars that are covered up with a large label, tear a strip vertically down the label so that you can see how much content is still left in the jar.

Get serious about saving pennies by using up the ketchup at the bottom of your almost empty bottle. Add a little water or vinegar and shake; then use the liquid to flavor soups, stews or salad dressings. *Submitted by Martha S.*

Use a glass jar to dry gloves and mittens. Pull each glove over the bottom of an empty jar and then position the jar upside down on a radiator or hot-air vent. Warm air will fill the jar and quickly radiate out to dry damp winter apparel.

Who needs a fancy set of drinking glasses when mason jars can do the trick? Forget about paper or Styrofoam cups for your next party and instead use your glass jar set. What a conversation piece! **Tip**: To keep a glass jar filled with hot tea or hot chocolate, slide the jar inside an old wool sock for insulation.

Save pieces of soap and keep them in a glass jar with just a little water in the bottom. After using paintbrushes, clean by swishing them around in the thick soap at the bottom of the jar; rinse with fresh water several times. This is a great artist's trick that works only with acrylic and other water-based paints.

Gift-in-a-Jar Vanilla Pudding Mix Recipe: Into a large bowl, blend 1½ cups (375 mL) instant dry milk, 1 cup (250 mL) sugar, 1 cup (250 mL) cornstarch and ½ tsp. (2 mL) salt. Measure ¼ cup (60 mL) into each glass jar. ENCLOSE THIS NOTE: with the following message: *Into a saucepan, add pudding mix, 1 cup (250 mL) milk and 1 tsp. (5 mL) vanilla. Stir until thick. Enjoy!*

Gift-in-a-Jar Potato Seasoning Recipe: Hold a pint canning jar at an angle, add ¾ cup (175 mL) salt, ¼ cup (60 mL) ground cayenne pepper, 1 tbsp.

(15 mL) white pepper, 2 tbsp. (30 mL) paprika, 2 tbsp. (30 mL) onion powder, 2 tbsp. (30 mL) garlic powder and 1 tbsp. (15 mL) black pepper. ENCLOSE THIS NOTE: *Shake and sprinkle (to taste) onto potatoes. Enjoy!*

 Gift-in-a-Jar Potato Soup Mix Recipe: Combine 2 cups (500 mL) instant mashed potatoes, 1½ cups (375 mL) instant milk powder, 2 tbsp. (30 mL) instant chicken bouillon powder, 2 tsp. (10 mL) dried minced onion, 1 tsp. (5 mL) dried parsley, ½ tsp. (2 mL) rosemary, ⅛ tsp. (1 mL) dried thyme, ¼ tsp. (1 mL) turmeric and 2 tsp. (10 mL) seasoning salt. Transfer ½ cup (125 mL) to each jar. ENCLOSE THIS NOTE: *Add 1 cup (250 mL) boiling water and stir until smooth. Enjoy!*

 Gift-in-a-Jar Coffee Creamer: In a jar, combine 1 cup (250 mL) hot chocolate mix, ¾ cup (175 mL) dry non-dairy creamer, 1 tsp. (5 mL) ground cinnamon and ¼ tsp. (1 mL) ground nutmeg. ENCLOSE THIS NOTE: *Stir 1 tsp. (5 mL) into coffee. Enjoy!*

 Gift-in-a-Jar Raspberry Vinaigrette Recipe: Lightly crush 1 cup (250 mL) fresh raspberries; place in a sterilized pint jar. Heat 2 cups (500 mL) white or wine vinegar to just below boiling point. Fill the jar with vinegar; cap tightly. Allow to stand for 2-3 weeks. Strain the vinegar, discarding fruit. Pour the contents into a clean, sterilized jar. Seal tightly. ENCLOSE THIS NOTE: *Pour onto mixed green salads, fruit salads or marinades for chicken. Enjoy!*

 End of the **Jar Waste Buster #1**: Use the last ¼ cup (60 mL) of store bought Italian salad dressing in the bottle to create another salad dressing by adding 2 tbsp. (30 mL) raspberry jam. Shake and pour onto greens.

 End of the **Jar Waste Buster #2**: Use the last ½ cup (125 mL) of salsa in the jar to make a yummy veggie dip by adding ½ cup (125 mL) ranch dressing to the jar. Shake and pour into bowl. Dip taco chips and veggies.

End of the **Jar Waste Buster #3**: Use the last bit of Nutella chocolate spread to create a flavorful toast topping. Add an equal amount of softened cream cheese. Spread onto toast.

 Brain-Up: How many single-serving jars of baby food does the average American baby eat in one year?

Answer: According to Gerber Products, the answer is 630.

 Did you know? Most bottles and jars contain at least 25% recycled glass. Glass should always be recycled; it never breaks down in the landfill.

Extraordinary Uses for Rubber Gloves

Give a big hand to versatile rubber gloves. Natural rubber latex gloves are made from the rubber tree. Rubber got its name from the British chemist Joseph Priestly, who noticed that it could be used to rub away pencil marks.

Sprinkle baking soda or cornstarch into latex gloves before putting them on. Not only will the powder help the gloves and your hands smell fresh, but they also assist gloves in slipping on and off your hands. **Tip**: Applying petroleum jelly to hands before putting gloves on will make your skin soft and gloves easy to remove.

- Spend a little more money on latex gloves and opt for fresh, comfortable gloves that include slip-resistant fingertips to help with gripping. Choose gloves lined with foam instead of the traditional cotton to help absorb more moisture and keep your hands from feeling sweaty. Cuffs on gloves should be long, making them easy to fold over and help prevent water from running back down your arms. **Tip**: For people allergic to latex, check out latex-free rubber gloves.

- Wear a pair of new rubber gloves to keep your hands clean and dry when greasing a cake pan.

- **Make Your Own Ice Pack**: Fill a rubber glove with crushed ice. Tightly close the wrist with a rubber band.

- Use old rubber gloves to make heavy-duty rubber bands. Cut strips on the round parts of both the wrist and fingers.

- Finger-pieces of rubber gloves can be used on the ends of mops and brooms to prevent them from sliding when leaned against a wall. Cut the tip of the fingers off and pull them onto the handle.

- Cut rubber gloves into long strips and use them as plant ties.

- Cut the fingertips off rubber gloves to make tiny finger puppets for entertaining children.

- Put on rubber gloves when trying to open jars, or cut up old rubber gloves and store the sleeve of them in drawers as grips to help open jars. Other methods for opening jars: Turn a closed jar upside down and bang it on the counter (being careful not to break the jar). Or place a wide rubber band around a jar lid and turn the lid; this will provide you with the grip you need.

- Instead of throwing out torn rubber gloves, wear when gardening. **Tip**: Keep old rubber gloves nearby outside to clean away spider webs.

- If you always wear out one rubber glove, start saving all the good gloves and by turning half of them inside out – you will gain a few extra pairs. **Tip**: Cut a few good fingertips off a torn glove and put them into other fingertip-torn gloves to reinforce them.

- Run out of little plastic bags for storing spools of thread? Cut the fingertips off rubber gloves and store spools of thread inside. **Tip**: Use glove fingertips as thimbles.

- To protect floors, cover the feet of chairs with the finger of rubber gloves.

- Instead of licking your finger when you riffle through a stack of papers, dollar bills or magazines, cut off the index-finger piece from a rubber glove for an ideal finger grip.

Reduce, Reuse & Recycle with Nylons

Quote of the Day: "A smelly foot equals fewer friends." – Reena Nerbas

Nylon first hit the market as toothbrush bristles, fishing line and surgical stitching. But on May 15, 1940, nylon stockings lined the shelves of New York City. By the end of the day, approximately 780,000 pairs had been sold. Soon the material and the hosiery made from it were synonymous and stockings, regardless of what they were made of, became "nylons."

Shoe Deodorizers: Fill knee-high stockings with unused kitty litter (I repeat: unused). Tie the ends and stick them into shoes overnight. Adding baby powder as an option. Reuse as often as you wish.

- When you've gathered pods from your garden for seeds, pull a nylon stocking over them and hang to dry. Once dry, shake and the seeds will fall to the toe of the stocking. Cut off, knot and store.

Store a few pairs of nylons in your car. They are better than rope for securing the trunk lid when hauling large items. You've got nothing to lose!

Old nylon stockings come in handy for cleaning sinks without scratching them. Just cut off the foot of an old nylon stocking, roll it up and use.

- To solve the problem of people washing their muddy hands in the house, place soap slivers in an old nylon stocking and tie it around the outside faucets of your home.

- Never again spend hours searching through carpet for a lost jewel or contact lens. When this does happen, cut a leg off an old pair of nylon stockings (no holes in the toe). Pull it up over the nozzle of your vacuum cleaner hose. Secure the stocking in place with a tight rubber band. Turn on the vacuum; carefully move the nozzle over the carpet, until you see the item on the nylon.

Fill old nylons with dry coffee grounds and tie off the ends. Hang in closets to absorb odors.

Amazing: If you are putting on a shirt and get deodorant on the outside, rub it with a nylon stocking and it comes right off.

- Eliminate static cling in clothing by rubbing the fabric on nylons. Or run the long side of a wire hanger over a skirt, or between your skirt and nylons or slip to get rid of static.

- A great way to store onions in the kitchen is with a pair of nylons. Place an onion in one leg, tie a knot, add an onion and tie a knot, repeat. The hose will allow air to get to the onions, making them last longer. To use individual onions, simply cut the hose one by one just below each knot. **Tip:** Store garlic and potatoes in the same way.

- When re-potting houseplants put a circle of nylons in the bottom of the pot before filling it. This stops soil from being washed out of the bottom each time you water.

- If you have a swimming pool, stretch a piece of nylon stocking over the skimmer and you will catch all those tiny particles that are often missed.

- Put the band from nylon stockings around a kitchen trash can to keep the trash bag from falling down inside.

- Buff your shoes, or just about any other surface, using a pair of nylons. Slip your hand into the leg and run your hand on the surface you want to clean. This works well for dusting too.

- Make a bag from clean nylons and keep it in the flour bin. Fill it with flour and use it when you need to sprinkle flour on a board when kneading bread or rolling pastry.

- Nylon is a strong lightweight alternative to rope. Use it to bundle firewood, old newspapers or to tie up packing boxes.

- Get organized! Store your nylons in sealable plastic bags. Sort by brand, size and color. Store each pair in their own bag to prevent snags.

- To extend the life of pantyhose, place them in a zip lock plastic bag, fill with water and freeze until solid. Thaw the bag at room temperature. Freezing hardens the fibers and lessens the chance of getting runs. *Submitted by Susan Rice*

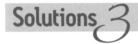

Solutions 3

Tips to Being a Good Fake

Unexpected (uninvited) company just pulled into the driveway. The house is a mess and there's nothing to eat. What to do? Of course none of these tips are based on personal experience!

- Company's coming and you are ahead of the game, toss a tea towel over your shoulder and slip on some rubber gloves. That way when they walk in, you just explain you were just in the middle of cleaning but "one must make a mess, to clean a mess."

- **Scoop & Swoop**: If time allows check the bathroom. Hair is the enemy! Wipe away all hair, faucets and counters. Throw dirty towels out of sight. Wipe your rubber glove along furniture that may be lined with pet hair (this is a fast way to collect fur and discard). Before they can ring the doorbell, run the gloves under cold water to get rid of the evidence.

- **Dirty Dish Upside-Down Trick**: You may have a counter of dirty dishes cluttering up the kitchen. Using the smallest dishes, place them in the sink. Put larger dishes upside down over the small ones, this will make it look like you just finished washing the dishes and they are drying in the sink.

- **The Microfiber Sprint**: If time allows, grab your microfiber cloth, dampen it with water and dust the piano, dark pieces of furniture and anywhere that dust is obvious. Do not mop the floor; doing so will tip off the visitor that you cleaned for company, unless you can work it into your "just cleaning" façade.

- **The Clean Oven Con**: If the inside of your oven looks like a science experiment gone wrong, reach for the aluminum foil. Pick up the bottom grill and lay smooth, shiny pieces of foil along the bottom. Do not use foil on self-cleaning ovens. **Tip**: Sprinkle cinnamon and a bit of water in a pan, pop it in the oven on low for 20 minutes. Your house will smell fabulous!

- The house is under control; now it's time to turn your attention to food. Always keep the following ingredients on hand in a box marked, "Really, Really Healthy Food" that way no one in the family will go near it. Include: 1 can each of tuna, peas, mushroom soup and 1 package of noodles. Combine all ingredients plus 1 can of water into a greased casserole bowl and bake for 30 minutes. Lunch is served! **Tip**: Other ingredients to keep on hand: tomato paste, marshmallows, canned fruit, instant pudding, cheese sauce, mashed potato flakes, frozen container of "Cool Whip" and headache medicine.

Marshmallow Dessert: Melt ¼ cup (60 mL) margarine/butter in a pot. Add in 40 marshmallows, stir until melted then add 6 cups (1.5 L) of add any kind of flaked breakfast cereal, e.g. Banana Bran, Just Right, Cornflakes, Special K, etc. Add 1 cup (250 mL) chocolate chips. Stir; flatten in 9x13" (23x33 cm) pan. Serve. Or instead keep ice cream in the freezer, scoop and top with fruit. Bam, dessert anyone?

- For pie filling that is runny, scoop into bowls and serve as individual crème de la something. Never apologize for anything you make, get creative!

- If you made a cake that stuck to the pan, return the cake to the oven for 3-4 minutes. Remove from oven and place the pan on a wet towel and wait at least 5 minutes before trying to remove it from the pan. A cake that has broken into a million pieces is now known as a "Trifle." Layer the cake pieces in a clear bowl with vanilla or chocolate pudding and whip cream. Top with fruit or chocolate shavings.
  Tip 1: Avoid white residue on a cake top by preparing the pan with leftover cake mix instead of flour.
  Tip 2: Homemade piecrust that is too liquidy should be wrapped in plastic and stored in the fridge for about 15 minutes. Add flour as needed.

- Runny cake icing can be resolved by adding additional icing sugar. Increase your chances of success by halving the icing and adding icing sugar to only one portion.

- Before giving up on over-whipped cream, fold in a few tablespoons of milk into whipped cream. If all else fails, serve as fresh homemade butter on bread or pancakes.

- Icing in a can will go twice as far when whipped.

- Whip cream is less likely to separate when a touch of unflavored gelatin is added to the mixture.

- The easiest way to smooth icing on a cake is to dip the metal spatula in warm water before frosting.

- When egg shell falls into a mixture, scoop it out with an eggshell instead of a spoon or fingers. The eggshell works as a magnet attracting broken pieces.

- If dinner rolls are a little hard, sprinkle with water and heat in the oven for 5 minutes to freshen.

- Salvage burnt rice by placing a piece of bread on the rice and cover with a lid. Leave for 8 minutes to soak up the burnt taste. Serve only the top layers.

- Break up lumps in gravy by whisking vigorously and putting through a sieve. **To prevent lumps in gravy**, blend flour or cornstarch well with oil or butter, or dissolve the flour completely in a small amount of cold broth or water before adding it to hot gravy. Add 1 tbsp. (15 mL) peanut butter to burnt gravy, add a little brown sugar to salty gravy and add 1 tsp. (5 mL) baking soda to greasy gravy (hopefully you won't need all of these tips at once).

- If sauce burns on the bottom of a pot, remove the pot from heat but don't stir. Place the bottom of the pot into a sink of cold water. Pour more than half of the sauce into a new pot and taste.

- Don't throw away overcooked vegetables – purée them and add milk to make a cream soup or pour the purée over cooked meat to create tasteful and healthy gravy.

- Potatoes peeled ahead of time and beginning to darken should be cooked with milk. Do not let the milk come to a boil, this will help the vegetables to brighten.

Remember: A housewarming is the final call for those who haven't sent a wedding present.

- **Anytime Gift Wrap Idea**: A unique wrapping paper for a new baby's gift is to circle the baby's birth announcement in the newspaper with a marker. Make sure the announcement is placed in a strategic position on the package.

- Sprinkle a few drops of cologne onto some used Christmas or gift wrap and use it to line your dresser drawers and storage boxes.

Green Idea: For the next wedding shower, birthday or Christmas party that you attend why not send or bring *Household Solutions*, the complete collection? Check out the collection at **householdsolutions.org**. Baskets include a variety of "green" products including *Household Solution* books, soap nuts, soy candles, cleaning clothes etc. **Note**: *Household* Gift Packages make wonderful contributions to Silent Auctions and handy gifts for real estate agents to send to clients.

Get the Most Out of Dinner Napkins

For those times when you want to make guests feel extra special, pull out the cloth napkins. A beautifully set table is enhanced by an artistically folded napkin at each place. Small touches send a message that you really value your guests.

Most paper napkins cannot be recycled (unless otherwise specified on the label), therefore, why not consider purchasing a beautiful set of cloth napkins? Cloth napkins do not waste trees, they look better and you get "new" ones every time you do your laundry.

Purchase inexpensive napkins to pack in lunchboxes. Wash them once a week with dishcloths and tea towels.

Tired of your cloth napkins? Recycle old napkins into **coasters**. Here's how: Choose the size that you want each coaster to be. Position a piece of felt underneath the napkin. Using pinking shears slowly cut through both pieces of fabric. Apply dots of glue to all edges of the felt piece. Make an X of glue dots from the edges through the center. Place the napkin piece right-side-up on top of the felt and press along the glue lines. Let dry for 24 hours. Don't wash the coaster for a week; air dry.

- **Handmade Napkin Option 1**: Using a loose weave fabric, run a row of stitching about 1" (2.5 cm) away from the ends on all four sides. Pull the threads until you reach the stitching and you are left with a wide fringe.

- **Handmade Napkin Option 2**: Pillowcases are available in a wide variety of colors and designs. Pick a color or design you like and start cutting napkin squares with pinking shears. Or sew ½" (1 cm) hem on each edge. You will have a new set of colorful napkins for a fraction of the cost of regular cloth napkins.

- For a fancy-shmancey table, your napkins should match the color as well as the fabric of your tablecloth. **Tip**: Dinner napkins are large in size and are not to be confused with luncheon napkins which are considerably smaller.

- **Crown Fold**: Fold napkin in half diagonally. Fold corners to meet at top point. Fold bottom point two-thirds to top and fold back onto itself. Turn napkin over bringing corners together, tucking one into the other. Peel two top corners to make crown. Open base of fold and stand upright.

- When folding a napkin design that must stand on its own, avoid using cloth napkins that are all cotton or linen because they have a harder time holding a crease and will begin to unfold. A more flowing or spreading design would be best for these types of material.

- Napkin rings can be made inexpensively with items you have in your home. Circle stems of long-stemmed silk flowers can make elegant napkin rings. Or use them as place-card holders by slipping a place card in the rolled-up stem. A length of paper-covered wire bent into a circle forms the base for a variety of decorative napkin rings. Add a tiny raffia bow and use hot glue to attach a small leaf and a nut for a fall themed napkin ring. Or braid together raffia and wrap around each napkin.

- Glass or metal bracelets can make fun and/or elegant napkin rings. Personalize napkin holders by purchasing alphabet beads from a dollar store and fixing them onto wire, tie and insert napkin.

- Use clothes pins as place-card holders or to keep napkins and plastic utensils together at a casual meal. Spray-paint the wooden clothes pins bright colors or colors to match the season.

- When setting the table, napkins should be placed on dinner plates or to the left of forks. **Tip**: Paper napkins are appropriate for a casual setting, folded and set to the left of forks.

- When sitting down to dinner, place the napkin on your lap. If it is large, unfold it halfway. Use the napkin to wipe your mouth and fingers as necessary.

- If you must leave the table before others, place your napkin in the seat of your chair, lightly folded, not wadded.

- At the end of a meal or function, the napkin is to be placed on the table to the left of the plate, lightly folded and not wadded.

- **Remove Lipstick Stains from Linen Napkins**: Apply petroleum jelly, smear into stain and then cover with dish soap before tossing into the machine. **Tip**: Dandruff shampoo works as well.

Flaming Hot Ideas

Since the discovery of fire, humans have used it for everything from cooking food, to lighting and warming our dwellings. Today we use fire and candlelight primarily to add ambiance to our homes or help celebrate special occasions like Christmas.

- **Candle safety**: In the year 2002, an estimated 18,000 home fires started by candles were reported to public fire departments. Half of home candle fires occurred when some form of combustible material was left or came too close to a candle; 18% of reports came because candles were left unattended, abandoned or inadequately controlled; 12% of candle fires occurred because people had fallen asleep, 5% were started by people (usually children) playing with candles. **Note**: Christmas Day had the highest incidences of home candle fires in 1999-2002. New Year's Day and Christmas Eve tied for second.

- Keep candlewicks trimmed to ¼" (1 cm) and extinguish taper and pillar candles when they get within 2" (5 cm) of the holder. Votives and containers should be extinguished before the last ½" (1.3 cm) of wax starts to melt. **Tip**: Nail clippers are great for trimming wicks.

- Twenty years ago, North American suppliers and manufacturers voluntarily stopped using lead based wicks in candle products; these generally remain unavailable to candle makers today. If you've recently purchased a candle, chances are it does not use a lead cored wick. Inspect your candle. Look closely at the wick; a metal core wick has a visible "wire" in the center. You may need to use your fingers to separate the core from the outer wrapping. If this wire core is not present, then your candle does not have a lead cored wick.

- Honey-scented rolled beeswax candles are not only easier to make than molded candles, but they also burn longer. Acquire sheets of pliable honeycomb-textured wax, in natural pale colors and in bright dyed hues. Supplies are available at crafts shops and dollar stores. Heat the beeswax with a hair dryer, position a wick on one end and roll the wax fairly tightly. Not only are these decorative but they also make nice gifts or gift toppers. **Tip**: Natural honey colored beeswax candles are a healthy choice because they contain no dyes.

- Create luminary lanterns out of tin cans and use them for decoration. Just drill a pattern of holes in cans and insert beeswax votives.

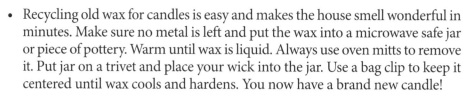

- To prevent wax from melting and sticking to the inside of a votive candle holder, pour a bit of water in the holder, then place the candle on top. If you forgot the water and the wax sticks to the candleholders, pop them in the freezer for an hour; the wax will chip right off.

- Store candles in the freezer overnight before lighting them. Not only will you have longer candle life but they will drip less.

- Recycling old wax for candles is easy and makes the house smell wonderful in minutes. Make sure no metal is left and put the wax into a microwave safe jar or piece of pottery. Warm until wax is liquid. Always use oven mitts to remove it. Put jar on a trivet and place your wick into the jar. Use a bag clip to keep it centered until wax cools and hardens. You now have a brand new candle!

- To repair a plastic toy, use the flame of a candle to heat the metal end of a knife. Hold the hot knife against both pieces of the toy to melt it back together.

 Green Tip: Most candles are made from paraffin wax, a waste product of the petroleum industry. When paraffin burns, benzene and toluene are released into the air (both are known carcinogens).

 The healthiest candles are beeswax and vegetable wax candles made from hydrogenated soy, palm and coconut oils. Soy candles are also a smart choice and are quickly becoming popular. The Canadian and American Lung Associations both caution against prolonged exposure to fragrances such as gel candles and soot for the very young, the elderly and those with respiratory diseases.

Green Tips for the Bathroom

- Purchase a high-efficiency water heater unit. Some new models heat water only when you need it, rather than storing hot water in a tank.

- Take a quick shower instead of a bath. A 5 minute shower, for instance, uses up to 50% less hot water than a bath.

- Avoid running the tap while shaving, brushing your teeth or doing dishes. Partially fill the sink with water and stop about 80% of that clean water from going down the drain – along with your money.

- Insulate water pipes to reduce heat loss. Insulate the first 6' (2 m) of the hot and cold water pipes from the water heater. A significant amount of heat travels through these pipes and can be lost, particularly through unheated areas such as basements and crawl spaces.

- For safety, don't place any pipe insulation within 6" (15 cm) of the exhaust vent at the top of standard natural gas/propane or oil-fired water heaters and never insulate plastic pipes. If you have an electric water heater, insulate the tank for further energy savings.

- **Dirty Toilets**: Do away with dirty toilets and harsh cleaners. Soak toilet paper with "Household Superstar Vinegar", see pages 18-19 of *Household Solutions 2 with Kitchen Secrets*. Press against the interior sides of the toilet. Leave overnight, wipe and flush.

Solutions 3

Keep Shower DOORS Looking New!

Question: If Donald Duck never wears pants, why does he drape a towel around his waist when he exits the shower?

- Reduce mildew growth on shower doors by leaving them open following showers to allow air to circulate.

- Although the surface of new glass shower doors seems smooth, they do have microscopic soft spots. Therefore choose your cleaners carefully; continuous exposure to chemicals may slowly dissolve the soft areas of glass away leaving behind etched glass (often a permanent condition). One option to prevent etching is to seal the glass surface so that it doesn't receive constant exposure to cleaners.

- Squeegee after showering. Doing this removes excess moisture and deters water spots that can be almost impossible to remove. Choose a plastic squeegee because metal may damage the door.

- Soap scum is difficult to remove and leaves a white film on glass shower doors. If possible change to liquid soaps. Talc in soap is responsible for the build-up of soap scum; the talc adds volume to soap without adding any value to it.

- To clean tracks and shower doors use lemon oil or hydrogen peroxide (let soak 5 minutes and wipe), or vinegar and water. Wipe with a soft cloth or cotton balls.

- Apply petroleum jelly to the inside of shower door tracks so that the door slides properly. **Tip**: Apply petroleum jelly to metal shower rods to keep them from rusting.

- To get soap film off vinyl shower curtains, spray them down with a solution of 50/50 vinegar and water. Next, wash them in the washing machine with another cup of vinegar and laundry detergent. **Tip**: For a better clean, wash shower curtains in the same load as towels.

Keep Shower INTERIORS Looking New!

Now grab your sponge and head inside the shower.

 SHOWER STALL CLEANER OPTION 1: Combine 1 tbsp. (15 mL) baking soda, 1 tsp. (5 mL) liquid detergent and water to fill spray bottle. Spray and scrub until clean. Rinse.

 SHOWER STALL CLEANER OPTION 2: Pour ½ cup (125 mL) dish soap into a bottle and fill the remainder with vinegar. Spray, leave for 20 minutes and wipe.

 SHOWER STALL CLEANER OPTION 3: In a ventilated bathroom, combine then pour into a spray bottle; ¼ cup (60 mL) vinegar, 1 tbsp. (15 mL) baking soda and 4 cups (1 L) water. Spray, leave for 10 minutes and wipe with a sponge.

CLEANING A CLOGGED SHOWERHEAD OPTION 1: Remove the showerhead. Fill a bowl with vinegar and place the showerhead inside. Leave overnight. Use an old toothbrush to scrub the deposits on the holes of the showerhead. Rinse with water.

CLEAN A CLOGGED SHOWERHEAD OPTION 2: Measure 1 cup (250 mL) white vinegar into a plastic bag. Place the bag over the showerhead and secure it with a rubber band, making sure the head is immersed. Leave overnight and then take it off the next morning.

 For mold growth that you find in the shower area or on grout.; combine 1 tsp. (5 mL) of vinegar, 1 tsp. (5 mL) 3% hydrogen peroxide with 1-quart (1 L) cold water spray and leave for 5 minutes. Wipe (test to make sure the vinegar will not damage shower fixtures or finish). **Note**: 3% hydrogen peroxide and vinegar create an even more powerful mildew killer when applied separately.

 Did you know? When ozone mixes with moisture in the air it forms hydrogen peroxide, which comes down in rain and snow. It occurs naturally in fresh fruits and vegetables, some coming from rain and some manufactured during photosynthesis. Hydrogen peroxide is also found in mother's milk, with an especially high concentration in colostrum (the first milk secreted, right after birth).

Solutions 3

Mold problems collect where the shower walls meet the floor or where the tub meets the wall. Cut rolled cotton into long strips and place around the perimeter. Soak cotton with undiluted vinegar and let stand a few hours. Remove and discard.

To clean copper and brass fixtures, sprinkle salt on half a lemon and rub over the surface.

- To break up stubborn soap scum from your shower fixtures, apply baby oil to a cloth and wipe the troublesome area clean.

- When unsealed, grout absorbs dirt, grease, water and whatever else comes near it. Seal grout with a sealer that repels moisture to prevent discoloration and keep it looking new. Scrub grout with a wet, soapy pumice stone.

- Install exhaust fans that automatically turn off once the proper amount of moisture is drawn out of the air. This way you reduce mold and mildew growth without leaving your fan on unnecessarily.

- **Wrinkled Silk Flowers**: To clean, put flowers in the shower and gently spray them with water. However, if the flowers are wrinkled then soak them upside down in a bucket of warm sudsy water for 15 minutes. Allow them to air dry and reshape them when damp. Another option is to let the steam from a hot shower draw out the wrinkles or use a heat gun (this is not as effective and more time consuming).

FOR THOSE WHO PREFER TO BATH

- Clean brown bathtub stains by combining 3% hydrogen peroxide with dish soap. Leave for 30 minutes and scrub. *Submitted by Mr. M. Dudar*

To remove non-slip appliqués and strips from bathtubs, saturate a cloth or sponge and squeeze hot vinegar over decals. Vinegar also removes stick-on hooks from painted walls. Soak a cloth or sponge with vinegar and squeeze the liquid behind the hook so that the vinegar comes in contact with the adhesive. Hot vinegar can also removes price labels and other decals from glass, wood and china. Paint the label or decal with several coats of white vinegar. Give vinegar time to soak in and after several minutes, the decal will rub off. Another option is to pour boiling water onto decals and lift with a plastic putty knife.

Greenways to Pamper Yourself

It's time to turn your home into spa central for the person who needs a break!

- Perhaps the most important part of the home spa experience is being sure you have uninterrupted quiet time. When creating the perfect spa experience, soothing music is an easy beginning. After that it is time for the perfect bath or shower followed by a few easy spa recipes using products from behind your cupboard doors.

- You'll be surprised at how lighting can create a stress-relieving mood. Lighting the room with candles will fill the area with a soothing scent and offer a very relaxing atmosphere.

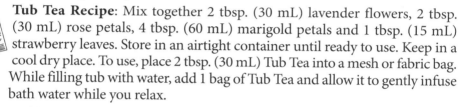

Tub Tea Recipe: Mix together 2 tbsp. (30 mL) lavender flowers, 2 tbsp. (30 mL) rose petals, 4 tbsp. (60 mL) marigold petals and 1 tbsp. (15 mL) strawberry leaves. Store in an airtight container until ready to use. Keep in a cool dry place. To use, place 2 tbsp. (30 mL) Tub Tea into a mesh or fabric bag. While filling tub with water, add 1 bag of Tub Tea and allow it to gently infuse bath water while you relax.

Bubble Nut Bath Recipe: In a bowl, combine ½ cup (125 mL) honey, ¼ cup (60 mL) gentle liquid soap, 1 tbsp. (15 mL) almond or vanilla extract and 1 tbsp. (15 mL) glycerin. Shake and add to bath. Or combine 1 tbsp. (15 mL) earth-friendly shampoo with ⅛ cup (25 mL) safflower oil; pour under running water. **Tip**: While you are at it, sprinkle a handful of rose petals onto the water.

Create-your-own Fruit Smoothie Hair Mask: In a blender, combine ¼ banana, ½ cup avocado, ¼ cantaloupe, 2 tsp. (10 mL) wheat germ and 1 tbsp. (15 mL) yogurt. Leave in hair for 10 minutes. Rinse.

I Can't Believe It's Not Butter, Face Mask Recipe: Combine 1 tbsp. (15 mL) regular yogurt and 1 tsp. (5 mL) soft honey. Apply to face 7 minutes. Pat and rinse face with a hot cloth.

Pinky Toe Milk Bath: In a saucepan, heat 5 cups (1.25 L) water and 2 cups (500 mL) milk. Remove from heat; add 3-5 drops peppermint essential oil. Soak feet for 15 minutes in the hottest temperature that feels comfortable. Rinse, dry and apply lotion.

Super Soft Sugar Baby Lotion: Combine 2 parts cooking oil with 1 tbsp. (15 mL) salt and 1 tbsp. (15 mL) sugar. Spread on hands and leave for 5 minutes; rinse in lukewarm water.

- Before a home spa manicure or pedicure, file nails and soak them in a bowl of warm water and 1-2 tbsp. (15-30 mL) lemon juice or olive oil to soften hands and cuticles. Let soak approximately 5-10 minutes. **Tip:** The final touch; purchase rhinestones from a salon and apply to toe nails after the pedicure.

Foot Powder: Blend ¼ cup (60 mL) baking soda with ¼ cup (60 mL) cornstarch. Add 8 drops peppermint essential oil and 8 drops tea tree oil. Blend for 2 minutes. Sprinkle onto feet or in shoes.

Foot Deodorizer and Soother: Soak feet in a tub of warm Jell-O.

Toothpaste: Combine: 5 tsp. (25 mL) baking soda, ½ tsp. (2 mL) salt, 4 tsp. (20 mL) glycerin and 10 drops peppermint or wintergreen. Store in a container and use daily.

Face Mask: Mash 2 tbsp. (30 mL) avocado; add 2 tbsp. (30 mL) honey and 1 egg yolk. Apply to face; leave for 15 minutes. Rinse.

Hand Lotion: Into a bottle, combine ¼ cup (60 mL) chamomile tea, ⅓ cup (75 mL) glycerin, 1 tbsp. (15 mL) vitamin E and ½ tsp. (2 mL) peppermint extract. Blend in small food processor until thick and creamy.

- Give yourself a spa treatment and save your face cream. Prevent cold cream from spoiling by storing it in the refrigerator. The added bonus is how cool it feels when applied!

Smooth Skin: Use a version of the secret recipe that Cleopatra used. Into your bath water drop 2 cups (500 mL) powdered milk. *Submitted by Angel L.*

- Shiny hair is possible with a bit of coconut oil. Rub oil onto your scalp once a week. Wash hair in the morning. *Submitted by Leslie D.*

- **Dry Hands:** If you have chapped hands or want to prevent chapping in the winter, rub the inside of an avocado onto hands.

Avocados are a wonderful hair moisturizer. Mix a peeled and chopped avocado with 2 tsp. (10 mL) wheat germ oil and 2 tsp. (10 mL) olive oil. Apply.

- Sugar is an abrasive and if you have very dirty, greasy or oily hands, rubbing them with sugar with clean them. Sugar also works well as a face exfoliant.

- **Yellow Teeth:** Strawberries have a natural bleaching effect on teeth. Rub strawberry pulp over your teeth and then rinse. **Tip:** Lemon peel rubbed over teeth is also a whitener.

- **Static Electric Hair:** Soak a hairbrush in water with a fabric softener sheet or apply lemon juice to hair before washing.

- **Heal Warts with Duct Tape**: When a wart appears, cover it with duct tape. Remove only to recover with fresh duct tape. Doing this will suffocate the wart and not only heal it but prevent new ones from coming. Healing time varies depending on the severity of the wart. If the duct tape is not holding substitute with book binding tape. *Submitted by Wendy Sidloski*

- To make your own hand soap, save slivers of soap bars and mix them in a bottle with glycerin. Shake with warm water and use.

Fade age spots by smoothing this combination onto skin twice a day: 2 tsp. (10 mL) plain yogurt and 1 tsp. (5 mL) honey. Let dry for 30 minutes and rinse. Results should become noticeable after 3 months.

Before composting coffee grounds, rub them on your hands to soften skin.

Soften face, feet and hair by combining a few drops of 50/50 Jojoba oil and Aloe Vera. Rub on hands or through hair, feels great! *Submitted by Sharon Nerbas*

To whiten yellowing fingernails, soak fingertips in 1 tbsp. (15 mL) 3% hydrogen peroxide and 1 cup (250 mL) warm water.

Little Barnard lost a tooth, but his gums won't stop bleeding, what should he do? Hold a dampened tea bag against the area until the bleeding stops.

Little Nicky has an earache but you can't visit the doctor until tomorrow. Soothe that ear by warming a few slices of onion in the microwave and laying them between two face clothes dampened with warm water. Lay his ear on the cloth and go back to dreamland.

Banana Face Mask Recipe: Combine ¼ mashed avocado, ½ mashed banana, 2 tbsp. (30 mL) plain yogurt and 1 tsp. (5 mL) wheat germ oil. Blend well and apply to face for 10-15 minutes. Rinse with tepid water.

Avocado Mask: For dry skin, mash a ripe avocado, pat on face and leave for 20 minutes. Rinse off with tepid water and smooth on a very thin film of apricot or almond oil.

To make a **light facial mask**, mix ¼ cup (60 mL) cornstarch, 1 egg white and about 2 tbsp. (30 mL) milk to a smooth consistency. Wash your face and neck. Rinse and pat dry. Apply a thin layer of the facial mask. Let stand 15 minutes. Rinse with clear water and pat dry.

To reduce large pores on the face, beat an egg white and add a few drops of lemon juice. Paint over your face and leave on for 20 minutes. Use three times a week.

Save tea bags, wet them and apply to eyelids for 15-20 minutes. This helps reduce puffiness and dark circles. Cucumber or raw potato slices also work well.

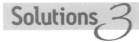
Green Cosmetic Homemade Body Lifts

Tired of being cooped up? Need a break from the cold air? Give yourself a home-made pick-me-up.

 Finger Lip'n Good Balm: In a microwave safe bowl, combine 1 tbsp. (15 mL) sweet almond oil, 10 fresh cranberries, 1 tsp. (5 mL) honey and one drop of vitamin E oil. Microwave until mixture begins to boil (may also be heated in a pan on stove). Stir well and gently crush the berries. Cool mixture for 5 minutes and strain through a fine sieve to remove fruit pieces. Stir again and set aside to cool. When cool, transfer into a small portable plastic container or tin. Smack your lips with this delightful balm and smile! **Tip:** Wear alone or over lipstick.

 Wind Beneath My Hair Shampoo: Combine ¼ cup (60 mL) liquid Castile soap, ¼ cup (60 mL) Aloe Vera gel, 1 tsp. (5 mL) glycerin and ¼ tsp. (1 mL) light vegetable oil. Store in an airtight container at room temperature and shake before use. Apply liberally to wet hair and let sit for a few minutes before rinsing well. **Note: Castile soap** is the general name for soap made with vegetable oils instead of animal fats. If you cannot find it at your local supermarket, try a health food store or online.

 Humpty Dumpty Back Together Again, Eye Mask: A great home remedy to get rid of puffy eyes is an egg mask. Mix 2 egg whites and a drop of witch hazel in a bowl. Apply to the face and under the eyes with a brush. This helps skin feel tighter and reduces swelling.

 Smoother Than a Porcupine Body Lotion: Combine 4 tbsp. (60 mL) vitamin E oil, 4 tbsp. (60 mL) grated cocoa butter, 1 tsp. (5 mL) honey and 3 drops vanilla extract. Melt over low heat. Add 1 tbsp. (15 mL) vodka. Cool and store in a plastic or glass container.

 No Coffee, One Cream Body Lotion: Stir together ¼ cup (60 mL) rosewater, ¼ cup (60 mL) glycerin, 2 tbsp. (30 mL) witch hazel and 1 tbsp. (15 mL) almond oil. Ingredients can be found at most drugstores or health food stores. Pour into an attractive bottle.

 Popeye Meets Olive Oyl Eye Make-up Remover: Blend together 1 tbsp. (15 mL) castor oil, 1 tbsp. (15 mL) olive oil, 2 tsp. (10 mL) canola oil. Store in a plastic container. Use with a cotton ball around eye to remove make-up. **Note:** Do not allow product to enter into eyes.

 Peppermint Patty Foot Bath: Combine ½ cup (125 mL) Epsom salt, 3-4 gallons (12-15 L) warm water, 5 drops peppermint extract, 3 drops tea tree oil and 3 drops lavender. Soak feet and dry with a towel.

Jailhouse Foot Bars: Mix together 2 cups (500 mL) soap flakes (check out grocery and health food stores) and ¼ cup (60 mL) water to form smooth dough. Add more water as needed, 2 drops red food coloring and 5 drops rose oil. Blend. Coat hands with vegetable oil and shape soaps with cookie cutters. Place soaps on a wax paper lined cookie sheet and let harden for 4-6 hours.

 Orange Presley All Shook-Up Face Mask: Did you know that besides being a great source of vitamin C, oranges have wonderful astringent properties that are perfect for oily skin? Squeeze ½ orange (with pulp) and 4 tbsp. (60 mL) cornmeal until a paste forms. Apply the paste as a mask to freshly cleansed skin. Leave mask on for about 5 minutes and rinse well.

 David L. Bowie Elbow Softening Lotion: Combine 4 tbsp. (60 mL) olive oil, juice of one lemon and 1 tbsp. (15 mL) honey. Store in airtight container. Apply to elbows 2-3 times per day.

 Flakey People Body Powder: Combine 1 cup (250 mL) baking soda and 1 cup (250 mL) cornstarch. Add 10 drops of favorite essential oil. Stir until fully mixed. Store in a shaker container.

 Oscar The Grouch Gives Back, Skin Soap: In a saucepan on low heat melt together 2 oz. (56 g) beeswax and 1 oz. (28 g) cocoa butter. Remove from heat and add 1 oz. (28 g) almond oil. Add 10 drops of favorite essential oil. Stir and pour into silicone muffin tin. Leave until set then remove from pan and use.

 Freeze and Nobody Gets Hurt Hair Spray: Remove rinds and chop 1 lemon (or an orange for dry hair). Place in a pot with 2 cups (500 mL) water. Boil until half of the initial amount remains. Cool, strain and place in a spray bottle. Add 1 oz. (28 g) rubbing alcohol as a preservative and then the spray can be stored for up to two weeks. **Tip:** If hairspray is too sticky, add more water.

 Two Eyes in the Same Hole Morning Body Scrub: Make a fresh pot of organic-caffeinated coffee, drink fast. Put grounds and 1 tsp. (5 mL) salt in a small bowl. Scrub mixture over entire body while in the shower. Rinse. Tone. Moisturize. **Tip:** Use grounds within 20 minutes of brewing before oxidation occurs.

 Whose Line Is It Anyway Face and Body Mask: Combine ¼ cup (60 mL) plain yogurt and 3 tbsp. (45 mL) honey. Separately purée 3 tbsp. (45 mL) canned (nothing added) pumpkin (or carrots). Add to honey mixture. Apply mixture to face and leave for 10-20 minutes. Rinse and apply moisturizer.

 Tip: Do you ever spray, hair spray in your face because you couldn't see the hole clearly?
Paint a dot of colored nail polish above the hole and you'll see it every time.

Pillowy Soft Nights

Not all pillows work well for everyone. A short trial of one week should be enough time to decide whether or not a pillow is providing enough comfort for a good nights rest.

- If a pillow is broken, badly stained or several years old, you are a candidate for a new pillow. A person who is not sleeping as well as they should be may have pillow problems; shoulder and neck pain are good indicators.

- Want to make a greener pillow choice? Choose pillows made from 100% recycled soda bottles. They are completely hypo-allergenic and covered in 100% unbleached cotton ticking.

- To tell if a polyester pillow is worn out, fold it over and place a weight on it like a mug. If the pillow stays folded it is broken.

- Check feather and down pillows for damage by folding the pillow over and squeezing out the air. If it pops open on its own it is still good. King size pillows should be folded in thirds.

- The best way to clean a feather or down pillow is by hand washing in a tub, gently and without agitation. Use fabric soap, not detergent. Dry the pillow in a dryer on the no-heat setting. **Tip**: To freshen up these pillows, add ½ cup (125 mL) vinegar when rinsing. Dry cleaning is also an option.

- Pillows that can be machine washed and dried on low heat should bathe in a water temperature of at least 135°F (57°C) to kill dust mites (unless otherwise specified). **Tip 1**: Put a couple of tennis balls in the dryer to fluff pillows. **Tip 2**: Freezing pillows outside or inside is another easy way to kill dust mites.

- **Wool pillows** may be dry-cleaned. Before attempting to wash wool pillows read the care instructions on the package. Wonderful qualities are attributed with wool pillows; they are cool in summer and warm in winter. On the other hand, they are hard, heavy and do not easily contour to the body.

- **Buckwheat pillows** conform to the body and give support to the head and neck. Buckwheat is natural and breathable but very firm (some may say too firm). Buckwheat is cool, dry and lasts about 10 years. It makes a sound as it is moved which may or may not be thought of as a disadvantage. The pillowcases can be machine-washed and tumble dried. Since it is almost impossible to dry soaked buckwheat hulls, cleaning the hulls is not recommended.

The inner liner rarely needs cleaning, when it does remove the hulls from the zippered opening and wash the liner in warm water and tumble dry. Replace the hulls when the liner is dry.

 Green Tip: Buckwheat hull and millet hull pillows are recognized as an environmentally friendly and orthopedically healthy sleep support. They are considered hypo-allergenic and will not attract dust mites.

- Use two pillowcases on pillows to resist the accumulation of dust and bacteria, sweat and other body fluids. Use a pillow protector as an additional barrier against dirt. Change pillowcases often because dirt penetrates the fabric and will end up on the pillow.

 Sweet Linens: Grind lavender buds, mint, dried scented geranium leaves or dried lemon verbena leaves in a coffee mill or blender. When changing the linens on the beds, sprinkle a small amount of this powder on the mattress (or mattress pad), then place the bottom sheet over and on the mattress. Since lavender has bug repelling properties, sleep time is not only sweet and relaxing, but reassuring as well. After placing fresh pillowcases on the pillows, sprinkle a small amount of this herbal powder inside the cases.

Caring for Popular Fabrics around the Home

A little maintenance can go a long way to preserve the life of fabric. Take care of spills and stains and address them immediately rather than allowing them to become ingrained.

- **Wool**: With proper care the natural qualities of wool can be maintained for years. If you give wool clothing a 24-hour rest between wearings it will shed wrinkles and return to its original shape. Hang woven wool garments on shaped or padded hangers. Store knits gently folded in drawers. Brush wool clothing to remove surface oil. Use a damp sponge for knits and finer fabrics. Refresh wool garments immediately after wearing or unpacking by hanging them in a steamy bathroom. Moisture from the steam removes wrinkles. If wool gets wet, dry the garment at room temperature away from heat. Brush with the nap. Remove spots and stains promptly.

 Cool Extra: A study done at the University of Sydney in Australia indicated that wool washed with a mixture of detergent and eucalyptus oil actually eliminated up to 95% of dust mites. The amazing thing is that they were able to do this at a lower temperature, thus preserving the integrity of the fabric.

- **Hemp**: Hemp has been used in the making of clothing, rope and canvas fabrics for centuries. Before the Industrial Revolution, most textiles worn throughout the world were made using hemp. Fabrics made from hemp are traditionally stronger, more durable and more insulating and absorbent than many other materials available. On average hemp fibers last 3 times longer than cotton. Traditionally, a coarser fiber was used to make canvas and rope; advances in breeding the plant have resulted in a much softer and finer fabric ideal for weaving into cloth for clothing. Never use bleach on hemp fabrics and avoid detergents containing Optical Brightening Agents (OBA's). Recommended water temperature of 120°F (50°C) is fine for most colorfast or un-dyed hemp fabrics. Tumble dry.

- **Cotton**: Cotton is probably the most common fabrics you have in your home. A natural fiber and is used in a wide variety of clothing and home furnishings, cotton is easily washed and/or dry cleaned. Cotton has a tendency to wrinkle very easily; however, cotton/polyester blends have gained popularity. Many people prefer the year-round "breathing" and lack of pilling of 100% cotton.

- **Silk** is a protein fiber, more similar to wool than to cotton and very similar to human hair. Remembering this will help when you think about how to wash or clean it. Silk is extremely strong, but repeated exposure to the sun will erode the fiber. As a result, silk fabrics are not the best choice for curtains and draperies. The colors in your silk will undoubtedly fade over time, even when permanent dyes have been used and they have been professionally set. Reds are particularly sensitive to running and fading. Store your silk away from exposure to light, especially direct sunlight. Washing silk may also cause excess dye to discharge. When in doubt, dry-clean the garment or item.

- **Rayon**: Some rayon fabrics should be dry-cleaned, while other types of fabric and garment construction can be hand or machine washed. For washable items, use mild lukewarm or cool suds. Gently squeeze suds through fabric and rinse in lukewarm water. Do not wring or twist the article. Smooth or shake out the article and place on a non-rust hanger to dry. Rayon sweaters should be dried flat. Press the article while damp on the wrong side with the iron at a moderate setting. Between wearing, rayon articles may be pressed with a cool iron. Steamers as opposed to traditional irons are perfect for rayon. Rayon is a popular choice for: blouses, dresses, jackets, lingerie, linings, pants, sport shirts, sportswear, suits, ties, work clothes, bedspreads, blankets, curtains, draperies, sheets, slipcovers, tablecloths and upholstery.

- **LYCRA**®: Originally developed as a replacement for rubber, LYCRA®, by DuPont, is remarkable for its ability to stretch many times its original length and then snap back to its starting size with no loss to its spring. Lycra® is never used alone, it is always combined with another fiber (or fibers) both natural or man-made. As little as 2% Lycra® is enough to improve a woven fabric's movement, drape and its knack for holding its shape. If the other fibers in the garment are machine washable and dryable, this should be the recommended method for cleaning. Dry cleaning is also an option. Avoid chlorine bleach when washing.

- **Satin**: Originally made from silk, most satin is now made with synthetic fibers. Follow instructions on care label: hand wash, machine wash or dry clean. Iron washable satin, inside out, while damp.

DID YOU KNOW?
Denim is recyclable and can be made into paper.

- **Nylon**: Nylon fabrics are extremely strong, lightweight, smooth and lustrous. It is also non-absorbent and has excellent wrinkle resistance. Often combined with spandex, nylon knits are very stretchy but recover their original shape. Nylon is used to make many items including lingerie, carpets, rainwear and tents. Machine-wash sturdy articles in warm water with an all-purpose detergent. Hand-wash lingerie and hosiery, using warm water and a light-duty detergent, or machine-wash in a mesh bag to prevent stretching or tearing. Tumble-dry nylon at a low temperature setting. Press at a cool temperature setting.

- **Acetate**: Acetate is made from cellulose and has a silk like appearance. Closely related to rayon, it has good body and drapes well. Taffeta, satin, crepe, brocade and double knits often contain acetate. Acetate is not very absorbent or colorfast and loses its strength when it is wet. If the care label specifies that the article is washable, hand-wash it in warm water, using a light-duty detergent. Do not soak colored items or wash them with white articles. Hang-dry acetate away from heat or direct sunlight. Press acetate at the coolest setting, on the wrong side, while the article is damp. **Note**: Nail polish remover and perfumes will permanently damage acetate.

- **Acrylic**: Many acrylic weaves resemble wool's softness, bulk and fluffiness. Acrylics are wrinkle-resistant and usually machine-washable. Often acrylic fibers are blended with wool or polyester fibers. Acrylic's biggest drawback is that it pills. Blends will do this less than pure acrylic. Wash acrylic by hand or machine. Turn garments inside out before laundering to reduce pilling. Wash delicate items by hand in warm water, gently squeezing out the excess. Machine-wash sturdy articles with an all-purpose detergent and tumble-dry at low temperatures.

- **Fleece**: The denser the fleece the better the quality. Gently stretch fleece and let it relax. Does it quickly bounce back to its original dimension or does it wave and ripple? High quality fleece has quick recovery. To give yourself a preview of how well the fabric will wear, rub the fleece roughly against itself, in a circular motion, on both sides of the fleece. If it looks a bit rugged, starts pilling, or distorts, it is a lesser quality fleece. High quality fleeces go through multiple shearing and velouring processes to reduce pilling. Fleece fabrics are predominately made from 100% polyester. To avoid unnecessary abrasion, launder garments inside out, separately or with similar garments. Use a powdered detergent in lukewarm water, gentle cycle. Liquid detergents may alter the effectiveness of the chemical treatment applied to some lighter weight fleeces. Hang dry and do not use bleach or softeners. Softeners have an adverse effect on the chemical finish that is applied to the surface of some mid-weight and heavy weight fleeces. Pressing is not recommended. Never place an iron directly onto the fleece as direct contact may leave a permanent imprint or melt the fabric.

- **Polyester**: A synthetic, manmade fiber produced from the polymerization of ethylene glycol and dimethyl terephalate or terephthalic acid. Some characteristics of polyester include crease resistance, an ability to dry quickly, shape retention in garments, high strength, abrasion resistance and minimum care requirements. Polyester is a very important fiber in upholstery fabrics. Before washing check the label but typically machine washing is acceptable. Avoid washing polyester in very hot temperatures as doing so may damage fibers.

- **Suede**: Suede by nature has got its problems when it comes to cleaning. The best way to deal with suede is to care for it well. Always clean suede before storing it. Suede can be brushed with a damp soft rubber or bristle brush and baking soda. Do not rub too hard and do it in a gentle circular motion or back and fourth. Never use chemical fluid or spot remover on suede as the color of the garment will run and leave light rings around the stain.

- **Velvet**: Velvet is usually made from rayon or acetate (a dry clean only fabric). Other velvets are machine washable, check the label and always launder inside out to protect the fabric from rubbing against other fabrics. If you need to have it pressed take it to your local dry cleaner or press it yourself by using what is called a needle board (available at your local fabric store). The top of the needle board has many needles protruding from the surface of a flat board. Put the needle board on your existing ironing board with the needles pointing upward, place your velvet fabric face down on the needles and steam press with an iron.

- **Fake Fur**: Clean once a year. Choose a professional dry cleaner that specializes in fake furs. The dry cleaner can remove stains left by food, make-up or spilled drinks. Regular cleaning serves to keep moths away. Wear a soft scarf inside the neckline of the coat to prevent body oils and make-up from collecting and causing a stain. Between cleaning, treat small stains on the fur and lining. Use a good cleaning fluid that is specifically for use on fur and fake fur. Test a small spot on both the fur and the lining. Use a blow dryer on the dampened spot to prevent a ring from forming. Store the clean fur on a padded hanger in a fabric bag. Don't enclose a fake fur in a plastic bag. Like real fur, fake fur needs to breathe.

Renew Your Fabrics

People started sewing as long as 20,000 years ago, during the last Ice Age. Archaeologists discovered bone needles with eyes, used to sew together skins and furs, dating back to this time. Perhaps it is time for us to get out a spool of thread and fix some stuff.

- Wrinkles will vanish easily if you keep fabrics in the freezer until ready to iron.

- Before mending a torn glove, drop a marble inside the fingertip. In the same way, before mending a torn sock push a light bulb inside the toe.

- Have you ever noticed a "W" or "S" on fabric care labels? The "W" stands for natural fiber and the "S" stands for manmade. "WS" stands for both.

- Fabrics (other than silk and wool) that have discolored due to washing with bleach can often be rescued. Boil the garments for 10 minutes in ½ cup (125 mL) washing soda to 6 cups (1.5 L) boiling water. Wash as normal.

- Silk and wool are two of the more difficult fibers to maintain. Care for them with caution and according to the label. If you are going to wash silk or wool at home use borax and do not put either into the dryer.

- To whiten ribbons and lace, soak them in fat-free milk for 2 hours before laundering.

- If you find that your thimble is slippery, secure masking tape to the inside.

- Lay clothes on grass to bleach. For an extra white result begin by sprinkling the fabric with salt and lemon before sun bleaching.

- Clothing will loose brightness due to the following factors: loads are too big, inadequate rinsing, too much or too little detergent and wrong water temperature.

- **Recipe for Whitening Cotton, Nylon and Polyester**: In a bucket or sink combine: 1 tbsp (15 mL) citric acid, 1 tbsp (15 mL) liquid detergent, 1 tbsp (15 mL) 3% hydrogen peroxide and ½ cup (125 mL) water. Let soak 20 minutes and wash as usual.

- When hanging clothing on the line to dry, spray lightly with water to prevent wrinkling.

- Spray fabric with vinegar to remove creases during ironing.

- Use soap slivers instead of expensive tailors chalk to mark fabric before sewing.

- Before hemming, mark a ruler with a rubber band to create an easy guide.

- Remember to take the time to check out the filter in your washing machine. Normally it is self-cleaning but on occasion it becomes caked with fabric softener and other residue. If this happens you will notice your clothing start to smell bad.

- In a pinch, use white thread colored with permanent black marker to make black thread.

- Getting married? Celebrating an anniversary or birthday? Have each guest autograph and sign a message on a square piece of linen instead of a guest book. Sew squares together and finish the edges with a narrow lace edging. In the center of the fabric write the occasion, guest of honor name(s) and date with permanent fabric paint. Make it a tradition to pull out the personalized table cloth on each anniversary of the occasion. *Submitted by Mrs. Elma Rose*

 Make Your Own Saddle Soap! Combine ¼ cup (60 mL) Ivory bar soap (grated), ¼ cup (60 mL) linseed oil and ½ cup (125 mL) beeswax. Melt over low heat and add ¼ cup (60 mL) white vinegar. Cool and use to buff leather. *Submitted by Trenton Witt*

 Recipe for Fabric Whitener: Combine 2 cups (500 mL) hot water, 1 cup (250 mL) baking soda and 1 cup (250 mL) hydrogen peroxide. Soak fabric for 30 minutes. Wash according to label instructions. *Submitted by Lynda Fehr*

- Tackle ring around the collar with a strong solution of cheap shampoo or apply mechanics hand cleaner. Scrub and wash as normal. Test on an inconspicuous area.

- Sticky glue on fabric can be cleaned using dish soap and water.

 Remove soot on shirts by applying Crisco to the area; wash with hot water.

- Put rubbing alcohol on a shirt that smells of grease. The smell of rubbing alcohol will disappear within a few moments.

- Sewing buttons on a shirt just got easier. Use a toothpick to help keep the buttons in place. Put a toothpick underneath the button and sew; doing this will prevent the button from being sewn on too tightly.

 Save sweet-scented flower petals from the garden. Dry and make small sachets to perfume your lingerie and your linen closet.

When washing plastic curtains or tablecloths, add 1 cup (250 mL) vinegar to the rinse water. The plastic will dry soft and pliable.

Instead of washing and drying baby's rubber pants normally, soak the pants in a mixture of glycerin and water for a few minutes. Rinse and hang to dry. The glycerin will help keep the pants soft and pliable.

To keep sheer curtains wrinkle-free, dissolve a package of unflavored gelatin in 1 cup (250 mL) boiling water and add to the final rinse.

If you continue to dry your washing outside even during the dead of winter, but don't like the frozen results, try this: Add 1 tbsp. (15 mL) salt per gallon (4 L) of water during the final rinse cycle of your machine. This will help keep clothes from freezing.

Rub grass stains on clothing with white chalk before washing.

Store an electric blanket by rolling it in lightweight cardboard. Wrap with string and stand upright in a cupboard.

To remove mildew from leather, clean with boiled linseed oil and a clean cloth.

If you tent has mildew spots, wet the area with water and rub a paste made from equal parts of soap and chalk on the mildew. Let dry in the sun until the mildew disappears. Rinse the area with a hose.

Using an old quilted housecoat for the inside of a baby quilt is a great way to recycle the housecoat and makes an inexpensive and light filling for the quilt.

Second-hand clothing is an excellent source of material and trim for making doll's clothes.

 ### Green Tips to Make the Laundry Room Energy Efficient

- Whenever possible wash and rinse in cold water using cold water detergent.

- Washing in warm rather than hot water uses 50% less energy and your clothes will come out just as well rinsed and, depending on the fabric, less wrinkled.

- Avoid over-drying clothes. Clothes should dry in 40-60 minutes. Better yet, hang clothes outdoors to dry when the weather permits.

- If you are buying a new dryer, look for one with a moisture sensor. It will turn off automatically when clothes are dry.

Nuts About Soap Nuts!

- Say so long to commercial laundry detergents and say hello to soap nuts. The soap nut (Sapindus Mukorossi) is the fruit from a tree which grows in India and Nepal. Soap nuts are all natural and safe! While the seeds of the soap nut fruit are used as detergents to replace artificial washing powder, the outer shell of the soap nut contains saponins which are good for treating skin problems. In India soap nuts are used in washing woolen and silk garments as well as a fabric softener, treatment for eczema, allergies and shampoo. Soap nuts are 100% renewable, biodegradable and can be composted after final use.

- Soap nuts have become popular as an environmentally friendly alternative to manufactured, chemical detergents. A few nuts are placed into a cotton drawstring bag, tossed in with a wash load and reused several times.

 Soap Nut Shampoo Recipe: Combine 6 cups (1.4 L) of water and 6-7 whole soap nut shells. Boil and simmer for 30 minutes. Strain the boiled nuts and pour the remaining liquid into a bottle to use as a shampoo on your hair.

- Check out your local health food store or go to: **www.householdsolutions.org** to get your first order of soap nuts.

Solutions 3

Take the Stink Out of Life!

Sometimes life stinks; no I mean it literally stinks. Commercial air fresheners work to mask smells and coat nasal passages with chemicals which diminish the sense of smell by deadening nerves. Avoid these products, instead, use all-natural air purifiers: **house plants**. Or try these easy recipes to diminish odors and add a fragrant, lovely smell to your home. May your home be filled with smells of fresh bread, fresh flowers and freshly cut grass.

STINKY TOWELS:

- Stinky towels often occur because towels dry too slowly. This happens most commonly to people who have dryers placed in their basements, due to higher humidity. The problem may need to be addressed by a professional as it could be a build-up of mold somewhere in the machine.

- If your washer has recently been installed, you will need to rule out the possibility that it was plumbed incorrectly. Incorrect plumbing may cause the washer to fill with nasty old water that should have drained out through the sewer pipe.

- Clean inside the seal surrounding the opening of the washing machine. Hair, fabric softener and a lot of other contaminants build-up in this area and if not cleaned properly can cause the machine to smell.

- Another common problem is the build-up of un-dissolved detergent underneath the machine drum. To get rid of this, run the empty machine on its longest, hottest cycle with vinegar (not detergent). If you do this once a month, it should prevent the problem from re-occurring.

- For front loading machines it's a good idea to mop up any excess water under and around the rubber door seal with a soft cloth after every wash and leave the machine door open to allow moisture to evaporate.

- If the washing machine is older, the timer and belt may need to be replaced because when the machine does not spin forcefully, the water will not completely spin out of the machine and water will sit in the drum.

- **Fabric Softener Substitutes**: (depending on accessibility some may be easier to purchase than others). Before laundering towels soak them in either 1 cup (250 mL): vinegar, borax, baking soda or washing soda and 12 cups (3L) hot water. Or combine 1 cup (250 mL) baking soda and 1 cup (250 mL) vinegar. Leave for a couple of hours before dropping the entire contents (towels and water) into the washing machine.

- Don't wash towels in one separate load; instead disperse them with other clothes. If you have access to a product called Pure Wash use that in conjunction with detergent. Pure wash is used to help eliminate smells developing in machines and can be ordered online at **smellywasher.com**.

Hang towels outside or lay on grass during rainy days; often rainwater alone zaps mildew smell.

- Oh, if you have a top end loading machine and you are using commercial detergents use **only** HE laundry detergent (not regular) and always the correct amount or less. You might even want to experiment by switching laundry detergents.

Juicy Fruit Room Air Freshener Recipe: Dissolve 1 tsp (5 mL) of baking soda in 2 cups (500 mL) of hot water; add 1 tsp (5 mL) lemon juice. Pour the solution into a spray bottle and spray any room in the house.

To purify and clean the air of any room burn 100% pure beeswax candles with 100% cotton wicks. They are said to purify and clean air while helping it smell great.

Cat Urine on Hardwood Floors: Combine 1 quart (1 L) 3% hydrogen peroxide, ⅓ cup (75 mL) baking soda and ½ tsp. (2 mL) dish soap in a container. Stir for 5 minutes and pour onto affected spots. The spots will foam; cover with plastic wrap and pile on heavy books. Leave for 1 hour and mop. Repeat three times. If smell remains sand areas and pour on the above recipe, cover with plastic wrap. Pile on books, leave for 1 hour. If smell still remains apply three coats of clear polyurethane. Although many people have reported great success with these techniques there are massive varieties of woods and finishes, test recipe on an inconspicuous area first.

Hockey Bag Horror Nightmare #1: Cut out one piece of corrugated cardboard 6" (15 cm) square. Sprinkle on a generous amount of peppermint extract. Stick into hockey bag and breathe easy.

- **Hockey Bag Horror Nightmare #2** (the continuing saga): Make your own sports equipment spray by combining 50/50 hydrogen peroxide and rubbing alcohol. Spray equipment and bag as needed, this helps zap smells and kill bacteria. **Note**: Wash hockey equipment regularly according to care labels.

- Deodorize hockey gloves by soaking them in water and scrubbing the inside (palms and fingers) with a bar of soap and an old toothbrush. Rinse, shake and air dry. **Tip**: Store a bar of soap in each glove when not in use.

Musty Wood or Fabric: Lay sprigs of eucalyptus inside or on top of furniture, or lay on fabric everyday for 3 days.

- **Once in a Blue Moon Drastic Cure for Smelly Automobiles and Homes**: Take the automobile to car care professionals and request the ozone machine treatment. The most effective way to get rid smoke smell or other foul scents, is to rent an ozone machine. The idea behind this little contraption is that it is made up of O_3 molecules as opposed to O_2 (oxygen). The third part of the oxygen is released into the air and gulps up any lingering odors. Use the machine according to directions on the box in a vacant building or vehicle.

Closet Air Freshener Recipe: Pour 1 package gelatin over ¼ cup (60 mL) water in a 2 cup (500 mL) measuring cup. Add ¾ cup (175 mL) hot water; stir until dissolved. Pour in 1 cup (250 mL) activated charcoal pellets (available at pet stores) and ½ cup (125 mL) salt. Let set. Place in an enclosed area.

Stinky Shoes: Lay a piece of plastic wrap inside each shoe. Put a drop of essential oil on a cotton ball and place it on plastic wrap. Or poke holes into the lid of an empty medicine canister and put essential oil perfumed cotton balls inside.

Tackle Skunk Smell on the Car Exterior: Pour 1 cup (250 mL) dry mustard into a bucket of warm water, mix well and splash it on the tires, wheels and underbody of the car. Your passengers will thank you.

Clean Air on the Rocks with a Twist of Lime Recipe: Combine 2 cups (500 mL) water, ½ cup (125 mL) vodka, ½ tsp. (2 mL) tea tree oil, ½ tsp. (2 mL) lime essential oil and ½ tsp. (2 mL) grapefruit essential oil. Spray as needed. **Tip**: This spray also helps deter cats.

Candy Cane Air Deodorizer Recipe: Fill a spray bottle with water and 5-10 drops of peppermint essential oil. Spray as needed. *Submitted by Joanne Villeneuve*

After cleaning the bathroom freshen the air by filling the sink with water, add a few drops of peppermint essential oil into the water to get rid of lingering odors.

Your microwave may look clean but still smell. Place a cup of cold coffee inside and heat it at maximum for 40 seconds. The smell will disappear.

Smelly kitchen got you down? Saturate a cotton ball with vanilla extract. Set it in a shallow container in an out-of-the-way place (e.g. window sill, on top of cabinets, on top of the fridge or inside the fridge). The family will think you just baked cookies.

After cooking, simmer a pot of water with lemon slices and parsley to mask food odors.

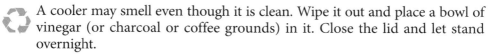
- Foul sulfur odor coming from bathroom sink? Your hot water heater may need a new Anode rod. Turn the water off and use a wrench to remove the old Anode rod from the top of the tank. Purchase a brand new Anode Rod and install.

 Forrest Gunk Air Freshener Recipe: "Life is like a box of chocolates, you never know what you're gonna get but at least you know it will smell good." In a spray bottle combine 2 tsp. (10 mL) rubbing alcohol, 8 drops cedar wood essential oil and 3 drops tea tree oil. Shake and spray. *Submitted by Trenton Witt*

A cooler may smell even though it is clean. Wipe it out and place a bowl of vinegar (or charcoal or coffee grounds) in it. Close the lid and let stand overnight.

- If you can't tell which perfume sample you like best, sniff coffee grounds in between each smell. This will cleanse your smell sense and get you ready for another whiff. *Submitted by Glenda, Orna and Rose Ly*

Little Catherine throws up on the carpet. What should you do? Blot with dish soap and water. Let sit until dry then vacuum. Sprinkle the area with coffee grounds; this will immediately absorb much of the smell.

Get rid of the smell of food on your fingers by rubbing them with dry mustard, wash in cold water.

To tackle a fresh milk spill in the back of a car. Sprinkle a box of baking soda over the offending odor and cover the area with newspaper, leave undisturbed for three days. Remove newspaper, vacuum up baking soda. Voilà: no more smell. *Submitted by Wendy in B.C.*

 Interesting Tidbit: A good way to tell how important cleanliness is to a particular restaurant, is to visit the bathroom. If the bathroom smells dirty and looks unclean, just imagine the kitchen.

Solutions 3

Help Conquer Household Laundry

After picking her son up from summer camp a mother noticed that he had on seven pairs of underwear. "Why are you wearing seven pairs of underwear dear?" she asked. The boy answered, "Well, you told me to put on a fresh pair everyday."

- If you choose to clean your sheer voile blouse, beaded top, fringed silk shawl or lace trimmed dress at home, place the articles in a cotton pillow case and knot it closed. Wash in cold water on a regular cycle. Hang to dry and steam iron or steam in the shower.

- To clean baseball caps without destroying their shape, place them on the top rack of the dishwasher and run through a complete cycle.

- If you don't have a sleeve board, insert a rolled-up towel into sleeves so they can be pressed without leaving creases. Or make your own sleeve board using a cardboard tube covered with soft fabric.

- Reduce wrinkles, preserve fabrics and avoid shrinking textiles by not putting clothes in the dryer on a heat setting. As soon as the wash load is finished give your shirts a shake and hang to dry. Also, lay sweaters to dry. Once the shirts and sweaters have air dried put them in the dryer on a cool setting.

Pit stains got you down? Make a paste of baking soda and water. Apply to yellow underarm stains and let sit. Wash in hot sudsy water.

Extra Tidbit: Speaking of pits, let's talk fire pits. Save your dryer lint. If you have a wood stove or fire pit, use lint as a fire starter rather than purchasing chemical laden fire starters.

- "Whenever I accidentally drop hair dye onto the carpet, I quickly pour the lotion from the home hair dye kit onto the area and dab it with a white cloth. The lotion is great at lifting the color out of the carpet." *Submitted by Hair girl*

- If you have really greasy or soiled clothes, pour 1 can of Coke into a hot bath of water and add in greasy or soiled clothes. Swish and soak. Wash as usual in hot water.

Make your own **Fabric Softener**! Combine 2 cups (500 mL) white vinegar, 2 cups (500 mL) baking soda and 4 cups (1 L) water. Allow fizz to subside and pour into a lidded plastic bottle. Shake and add ¼ cup (60 mL) to each load.

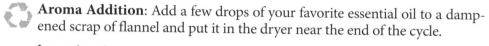

 Black clothing tends to look brown after several washings. To restore the black color, add coffee or strong tea to the rinse water.

- To iron embroidered linens, place the linen with the embroidered side down over a white terry towel then press (wrong side-up). This will help preserve the direction of the stitching without flattening it. You can also do this in reverse; first lay the embroidered side up and then put a terry towel on top and press.

- Keep a few hangers on a small bar or hook in your laundry room so you can hang wrinkle-prone items up as soon as you remove them from the dryer.

Aroma Addition: Add a few drops of your favorite essential oil to a dampened scrap of flannel and put it in the dryer near the end of the cycle.

- Invest in a 3-compartment laundry sorter to make easy work out of keeping clothes separated. Separate by color as you put clothes into the hamper and save the step of going through hampers and hampers full of laundry an item at a time. By sorting-as-you-go, when you see a full compartment in your hamper, it is simply time to wash the load.

- For grease stains on fabric, apply talcum powder to both sides of the spot. Dab and let stand overnight, wash as usual.

- When dealing with wine stains on fabric that remain after being to the dry cleaners, try this little trick. Pour dish soap onto the stain and soak with 3% hydrogen peroxide. Check results everyday, may take up to 3 days to disappear. Test on an inconspicuous area first.

- Nail polish on carpet? Apply shaving cream, use a small amount of water and work the solution into a lather. Dab and rinse.

 SOAP

No one knows exactly when soap was discovered, but according to Roman legend, soap was named after Mount Sapo, an ancient site of animal sacrifices. Following an animal sacrifice, rain would wash the animal fat and ash that collected under the ceremonial altars down the slopes to the banks of the Tiber River. As women washed their clothing in the river they noticed that if they washed their clothes where the ashes floated their clothes became clean.

When purchasing soap, choose a product that is made with non-synthetic, plant-based ingredients, biodegrades safely and is completely non-toxic.

Solutions 3

Grass Stains on Pants: make a paste of white granulated sugar and water and spread it over affected area. Let sit for 1 hour and wash as usual.

- Since Betsy started dating you have mysteriously noticed an increase in antiperspirant stains on her clothing. Remove antiperspirant marks on dry clean only garments by dabbing with rubbing alcohol. (Test on an inconspicuous area first).

Adding a couple of clean, dry bath towels to a load of drying helps cut down the drying time because the towels absorb the excess moisture.

To save drying time, get rid of extra water from heavy items such as towels and flannelette sheets by putting them through an extra spin cycle in the washing machine. The spin cycle uses less energy than the dryer.

Hi Reena,

I have always cleaned my dryer screen after each load in order to promote efficiency of the drying process, long-life of the heating element and safety. But I find that there is some embedded lint that does not seem to budge, even after I have vacuumed the screen and then used a toothbrush (dry and then wet) to try and remove it. I have even tried using a toothpick and although this method seemed to be more successful, it was far too time consuming. Is there another more effective and easier method I can use to remove the embedded lint? I would be grateful for any helpful advice. Thanks, Ann

Hi Ann,

Fabric softeners and other laundry products do leave a thin layer of film on dryer sheets. Soak the lint dryer screen in a bath of warm, soapy water for about 15 minutes; then use a stiff scrub brush/nail brush to remove the lint. Rinse all the soap from the screen in 50/50 vinegar and water and allow airing dry overnight prior to use.

Reader's Comment: I use the powdered laundry detergent that is sold in plastic pails. It is such a struggle to get the lid off with each use, so now I just rest the lid on top of the pail. Needless to say, this allows moisture in, causing a problem with clumping. I decided to toss in a couple of packages of the silica gel that is sold with shoes. It keeps the laundry detergent dry and works amazingly well! *Submitted by Veronica S.*

Go Green at the Office

We can compost and conserve all we want but as soon as we hit the office, we often opt for triplicate-printing, paper-cup-squashing and running-our-computers-all-night.

The average worker in North America goes through 10,000 sheets of copy paper a year. Make it a habit to print on both sides and/or use the back side of old documents for faxes, scrap paper, or drafts. Avoid color printing and print in draft mode whenever feasible. Try to reuse every scrap of paper, even if it is written on, before recycling it. You can even go one step further and buy writing pads that made with recycled paper which cost a fraction of the price of new.

Some paper use can't be avoided, so use recycled paper and envelopes that have been processed and colored using eco-friendly methods. Pens and pencils can also be made from recycled materials and refillable pens and markers are preferable to disposable ones. Buy in bulk so that shipping and packaging waste are reduced and reuse shipping boxes. Recycling printer cartridges is often free and recycled replacements are cheaper than new ones.

Keep recycle bins next to wastebaskets and copiers to remind people to recycle. Instead of buying notepads, make your own out of recycled paper.

Instead of letting computers and other electronics power down into sleep mode, institute a mandatory shut off of all computers and electronic devices every night after work. Use power strips instead of wall outlets and switch off the power strips at the end of the work day. **Tip**: Power strips are less expensive than surge protectors and often pay for themselves in six weeks.

A green plant in your office will do wonders for the atmosphere and produces vital oxygen for you through photosynthesis.

Switching from incandescent bulbs to energy-efficient compact fluorescents delivers outstanding efficiency (up to 75% energy savings for Energy Star qualified lights). That translates into significant cost savings as well as waste avoidance since compact fluorescents can last over 10 times longer than incandescent bulbs. These bulbs fit standard fixtures and deliver excellent natural light.

Use timer switches to turn off vending machines and copiers when the office is closed.

Bag up the garbage from your shredder and take to the recycling center.

Buying a new computer? Choose a laptop; it uses about 6 times less electricity than a desktop, according to *The Carbon Buster's Home Energy Handbook*.

Solutions 3

More than 8 billion disposable cups are thrown out every year in Canada. Buy a reusable coffee mug and take it with you on your morning coffee break.

North Americans buy more than 8 billion gallons of bottled water and some 22 billion empty plastic water bottles are thrown away each year, according to National Geographic magazine. If you really can't stand using plain old tap water, get a filter, such as Brita and fill up a reusable neoprene bottle for your H_2O to go.

A home-packed lunch is undoubtedly cheaper and produces less solid waste than take-out food. Rather than buying plastic containers, reuse takeout containers before throwing them into the recycling bin. Reuse bread wrappers and other plastic packaging instead of buying plastic wrap or aluminum foil. Keep reusable spoons, forks and chopsticks in your desk instead of disposable.

Before purchasing new office furniture for your home, check your storeroom to see if there is something that can be used. Just because something isn't called a "desk" doesn't mean it can't be used as one. A flat door placed on a pedestal or saw horse type legs are an option. Or use short bookcases turned outward as the supports for a new desk.

In the office washroom use hand-dryers rather than paper towels. Use biodegradable soaps and cleaners.

Poor indoor air quality can be very expensive for any size business when employees develop environmental sensitivities and require sick leave. New materials should be given adequate ventilation after being installed to reduce exposure to chemical off-gasses; an example would be to leave windows open overnight after carpet installations. **Tip**: Companies can invest in allergen filters for central air offices, replacing every three months or as directed.

Offices use tons of batteries to power things like calculators and hand-held massage devices. When possible, buy rechargeable batteries so they can be used time and time again and ultimately, create less waste. According to rechargeable battery makers, rechargeable batteries have 32 times less impact on the environment.

 DID YOU KNOW? A new poll by Harris Interactive sites that while most North Americans say that they have gone green at home, only half try to be greener at work.

It takes one, 35' (10.7 m) tall tree to make a stack of paper 6' (1.8 m) tall. Recycling approximately 1 ton of newspapers saves 17 trees.

Index

Solutions 3

Brick – **Fireplace Cleaner recipe, 122**; paint stain removal, 37; replace damaged, 37; sealing, 37; white salt residue removal, 37
Bubble Wands – homemade, 41
Buffer – with nylons, 133
Bugs – in food, 78; **Insecticide recipe, 55; Repel Bugs recipe, 26**; spray, 55
Burns – treating, 57, 120
Butter – usage, 119; wrappers for baking, 111
Butterflies – feeder, 58
Cabbage – planting, 48-50; retaining red color, 117
Cabinets – best green type, 99; cleaning, 33; cleaning fronts, 100; organizing when painting/refinishing, 105
Cakes – 113-114; broken, 135; cupcakes, 113; decorating, 114; greasing pans, 113; oven temperature, 113; prevent from falling, 113; stuck to the pan, 135; white residue, 135
CancerSmart© – 3.0 The Consumer Guide, 13
Candles – 139-140; Beeswax, 139; melting, 140; lanterns, 139; recycling, 140; safety, 139; storing, 140; trimming, 139; vegetable wax, 140; wicks, 139
Cankerworms – controlling, 69
Carbon Monoxide Detector – care of, 33
Carcinogens – 12-13
Carpets – Beetles, 77; choices, 93; cleaning, 85; finding lost items, 132; finger test, 93; **Freshener recipe, 22**; lining drawers, 94; measuring, 91; nail polish, 165; purchasing, 93; removing hair dye, 164; **Steam Cleaner recipe, 123**; texture quality, 93; VOC emissions, 94
Carrots – nematode infection, 51; planting, 48, 49; root fly repellent, 49; seed germination, 48
Cars – buffer, 22; recycling, 20; rid of smells, 162; securing trunk lid, 132; skunks smells, 162
Cast Aluminum – furniture, 43; painting, 43
Castile Soap – 122, 148
Catnip – Oil mosquito repellent, 68; repel cockroaches, 77
Cats – bowls, 61; litter pan, 62, 63; **Snack recipe, 60**; using scratching post, 62, 63
Cauliflower – planting, 48, 49; soaking, 127
Cedar Furniture – care, 42; cleaning, 42; painting, 42
Ceiling Fans – dusting, 85; fixing noise, 89; reduce energy, 20
Celery – planting, 48-50; save leaves, 117; storing, 117
Cellphones – germs, 9; recycling 20
Cereal Boxes – make clipboards, 89
CFC-free Claims – products, 16
CFL Light Bulbs – save power, 20
Chairs – floor protectors, 131
Chamomile – fly, mosquito repellent, 50; planting, 50
Charities – recycling, 20
Cheese – cleaning graters; 105; softer, 111
Chemical Sensitivity – about, 18; symptoms, 18
Chemicals – eliminating, 12; exposure, 18; Chemical-Free, 15; leaching, 11; polluting, 11; Sensitivity, 18; testing, 11

Chicken – fried, 110; roasted, 110; roast rub, 25; stuffing, 118
Children – activity, 40; **Best Bubble Making Solution, 41**; bicycle helmet use, 40; bicycle riding clothing and conditions, 40; **Bubble Wands, 41**; puppets, 130; safety, 40; sandbox buffer, 40; **Sidewalk Chalk recipe, 40; Sidewalk Chalk Molds, 41; Yummy-in-your-Tummy Homemade Ice Cream – recipe, 41**
China cups – removing stains from, 107
Chipmunks – about, 58; deterrents, 58; lure, 58
Chives – planting, 49
Christmas – storing decorations, 87; watering trees, 127
Chrome, Glass and Porcelain – polish, 31
Cinnamon – combat plant infections, 51
Cleaners – absorption, 11; carcinogens, 12; claims, 15; eliminating, 12; for hardwood floors, 95; hard to reach places, 121; ingesting, 11; ingredients, 12; safety, 11; silica, 12; testing, 11; using biodegradable, 99
Clipboards – making, 89
Closets – **Air Freshener recipe, 162**; deodorizer, 132; don't heat, 39; garment protectors, 86; removing odors, 84
Cloth Diaper Whitener – recipe, 123
Clothesline – saves power, 20
Clothing – freshener, 30; removing deodorant, 132; removing lint, 90; removing static cling, 133; second-hand 158
Club Soda – for houseplants, 120
Coasters – making, 137
Cockroach – poison, 22
Cocoons – controlling, removing, 69
Coffee – cleaning grinder, 106; closet deodorizer, 132; cloudy coffee, 120; filters, 100; **Gift-in-a-Jar Coffee Creamer, 128; Iced Coffee, 127**; switch off maker, 100; reusable mug, 168
Collecting – materials for recycling, 20
Companion Planting – benefits, 48-50; spacing, 48
Company Coming – 134-135
Composting – 46; apartment size, 47; food waste, 20; for the garden, 20; ingredients, 46; in soil, 46; layering, 46; liquid manures, 44; materials, 46; organic fertilizer, 46; plant food, 46; ratio, 47; size, 46; Worm Vermicomposting system, 47
Computers – cleaning keyboard, 90; recycling, 20; shutting down, 167
Consumers – caring, 14-17; informed, 12-17; exposure, 12; misled, 14; well-intentioned, 14
Containers – reuse, 20; for recycling, 20
Cookbooks – protecting, 105
Cookies – 113-114; decorating sugar cookies, 114; dough gluey, 113; flouring baking sheets, 113; lifting from pan, 113; perfectly shaped, 113; pre-shaped cookie dough, 113; using juice cans, 113; using paper stencils, 114

Solutions 3